Listen To Win

Listen To Win

A Manager's Guide To Effective Listening

Curt Bechler
Denison University
Granville, Ohio

and

Richard L. Weaver II
Bowling Green State University
Bowling Green, Ohio

MasterMedia Limited • New York

Published 1994 by MasterMedia Limited

MASTERMEDIA and colophon are registered trademarks
of MasterMedia Limited.

Library of Congress Cataloging-in-Publication Data
Bechler, Curt.
  Listen to win : a guide to effective listening / Curt Bechler
  and Richard L. Weaver II.
        p.   cm.
  Includes bibliographical references.
  ISBN 1-57101-002-5
    1. Listening. 2. Interpersonal relations. 3. Interpersonal communication.
4. Communication in management.   I. Weaver, Richard L., 1941–.
II. Title.
BF323.L5B43 1994
658.4' 095—dc20   94-1744

Book design by Alan L. Marks
Production services by Lynn & Turek Associates, New York
Manufactured in the United States of America

10 9 8 7 6 5 4 3 2 1

CONTENTS

Preface   ix
Introduction   xiii

PART ONE
  WHY DO MANAGERS NEED A BOOK ON LISTENING?
  1 Why Can't You Get Information On Listening?   *3*
  2 What's In This Book For You?   *6*
  3 What Does It Take To Change Habits?   *9*
  4 Where Can You Begin?   *16*

PART TWO
  WHAT DO MANAGERS NEED TO KNOW
  ABOUT THE LISTENING PROCESS?
  5 What Does Listening Require You To Do?   *25*
  6 Why Must You Understand The Process Of Reduction?   *29*
  7 What Happens When Information
     Is Sent Through Filters?   *34*
  8 How Do The Three Phases Of The Listening Process
     Affect You?   *40*

PART THREE
  HOW CAN MANAGERS LISTEN
  TO IMPROVE THE WORK ENVIRONMENT?
  9 Why Is Listening Related To Your Business Survival?   *49*
  10 Why Is Listening Related To Your Survival?   *53*
  11 Why Do You Need Ways To Create
     A Positive Listening Environment?   *56*
  12 How Can You Combat Poor Listening Behavior?   *61*

PART FOUR

HOW CAN MANAGERS LISTEN
SO EMPLOYEES WILL SPEAK?

13 How Do You Create Listening Problems?　*71*

14 How Can You Use Active Listening
For Listening Effectiveness?　*74*

15 How Can The H.E.A.R. Method
Help You Listen Better?　*77*

16 How Can You Use A Positive Past
To Forecast A Positive Future?　*81*

17 How Can You Avoid The Barriers
To Effective Listening?　*84*

PART FIVE

HOW CAN MANAGERS LISTEN
SO SUPERVISORS WILL SPEAK?

18 What Is Your Key To Upward Mobility?　*93*

19 How Do You Discover What Your Supervisor
Thinks Is Important?　*97*

20 Why Listen When No One Expects You To?　*103*

PART SIX

HOW CAN MANAGERS FIND THE "TRIP WIRES"?

21 How Can You Use Trip Wires
To Increase Effectiveness?　*109*

22 How Can You Find A Trip Wire In Context?　*113*

23 How Can You Use Past Experiences
As Positive Trip Wires?　*115*

24 How Can You Use Emotions And Time
As Trip Wires?　*118*

PART SEVEN

HOW CAN MANAGERS LISTEN
TO COPE WITH CONFLICT?

25 How Can You Listen To Yourself
To Control Your Emotions?　*123*

26 How Can You Analyze Everyone's Goals?　*127*

27 Why Doesn't Time Get You The Results You Want?　*131*

28 How Can You Become A Peacemaker?　*135*

PART EIGHT

HOW CAN MANAGERS LISTEN IN MEETINGS?

29 What Are Your Barriers To Listening In Meetings? *145*

30 How Can You Use Listening To Build
Teamwork In Meetings? *149*

31 What Three Listening "Rights" Do You Need
To Develop A Productive Discussion? *154*

32 How Can You Use Internal Synergy
In One-on-One Meetings? *158*

33 How Can You Use External Synergy
To Stimulate New Ideas? *162*

PART NINE

HOW CAN MANAGERS LISTEN
FOR PERSONAL GROWTH?

34 What Does It Mean To "Listen To Yourself"? *169*

35 What Strategies Can You Use For Personal Change? *172*

36 How Does Listening To Yourself Relate
To Effectively Listening To Others? *176*

References *183*
About the Authors *185*

PREFACE

First and foremost, this is a book about getting along with people. It is a book about learning to live with others, whether they are a spouse, child, friend, coworker, or boss. While this book is aimed at the workplace and managers who occupy that workplace, listening effectively is also a skill that applies no matter who you are, what you do, or where you are. The skills discussed here apply to getting along effectively and successfully with others. This is a people-oriented book about a people-oriented process.

Etched into the minds of Americans is the tearful statement of Rodney King during the Los Angeles riots, "Can't we just get along?" As the world we live in seems to get progressively smaller, as the job market shrinks, as multiculturalism grows, as people become more intimately and directly interconnected with others, those who succeed will be those who know how to get along with others regardless of circumstances or background. The people who succeed will not only have the good product or the good idea, they will have learned that good ideas, effective decisions, and winning solutions come through the understanding of, and sensitive dealing with, the needs of others.

There is an old negotiating story that illustrates what we are talking about: A mother had two daughters. One day the mother discovered the daughters arguing over who would have the last orange. Rather than listen to her daughters' arguments, the mother simply took the orange, calmly cut it in half and gave each daughter a piece. Problem solved. This appears to be a happy, agreeable, and appropriate solution, right?

It may appear to be happy, agreeable, and appropriate, but consider this: The first daughter took her half of the orange, ate the insides, and threw away the peel. The second daughter took her half, used the peel to make a cake, and threw away the insides. The mother's solution, while ending the argument, did not address the issues. Most effective solutions begin with something as simple as learning how to listen.

Learning to value someone else's opinion by listening to them is not only the key to good solutions, but it is also the key to successful long-term business relationships. Just about anybody who is halfway articulate can give a reasonably good sales pitch. A reasonably good sales pitch, for the most part, will help make a sale in the first round. But the secret to success is not in the first sale alone. It is found when that first-sale customer comes back to you for the second, third, tenth, and twentieth time. Success is in the repeat business.

Why would a first-sale customer come back a second, third, tenth, or twentieth time? Obviously because these customers are getting what they want. That is because you are giving them what they want! How do you know what they want? Because you listen effectively. You are listening for their needs. This enables you to anticipate both their needs and their wants. It gives you that extra edge, while telling them they are important. This is why listening is a people-oriented process. Throughout the book, we demonstrate this with a variety of stories and illustrations (often, individual and business names have been changed to honor confidentiality).

We have a friend, named Tom, who found himself competing in a job with a gentleman, named Paul, who was extremely articulate and aggressive. In the beginning, when they were both on a customer call, Tom found himself overshadowed by Paul, who would immediately engage the customer and dominate the conversation, not giving Tom an opportunity to get a word in edgewise. Tom was left to listen.

Tom began to make an interesting observation. When he would eventually jump into the conversation, his comments were readily heard by the customer because he addressed exactly what the customer had been saying. Paul would focus on his own needs, trying to convince the customer to buy the product that Paul believed was the best. Tom found that what the customer needed and what Paul needed were often two different things. By listening, Tom identified the customer's needs and followed up with questions and suggestions that addressed precisely those needs. Tom used effective listening.

Customers, as we all know, vote with their wallets. What Tom thought would be a difficult competition with Paul turned out to be a lesson in getting ahead through effective listening. This is a lesson most of us can learn. People, regardless of their background, education, status, or position, do not listen well.

All this may sound as if we are focusing on listening from a dollars-and-cents perspective. Actually we are focusing on getting the most out of life. Life becomes easier, more enjoyable, and more rewarding when we don't have to have all the answers. We don't have to control all the observations, we don't have to know all the solutions, and most important of all, we don't have to do all the talking!

An amazing thing occurs when we become comfortable with ourselves. We find that we don't have to convince others of our own worth. We don't have to demonstrate our superior knowledge. We don't have to prove we know all the answers. When we become comfortable with ourselves, we can begin to see others' worth. When we begin to see worth in others, true listening begins.

Seeing worth in others is the kind of success we are talking about in this book. This book is not about making money, although listening successfully may result in your making more money. This book is not about getting a promotion, although success in listening may result in promotions. This book is not about business security, although listening successfully may result in greater business security. The kind of success we're talking about in this book is being comfortable with ourselves, faults and all. Once we are comfortable with ourselves, we will be able to value and be comfortable with others. This, we feel, is the bottom line. That's why we say this is a people-oriented book about a people-oriented process!

Most of us think of listening as something passive, something you just sit back and do. Most of us think of listening as a process that requires little energy and effort. As you are about to read, listening effectively is far from passive. This book will demonstrate that listening means action. It means doing the unexpected. It means taking risks. And it means hard work! We believe this is why so many people fail to listen well!

What you are about to read is not a shopping list of ten easy steps to better listening. It is a way of life, a mind-set. It is about a personal transformation in the way each of us approaches communication situations. This is a story of how to get along with people, how to connect with them, how to get the best from them, and how to empower them. You will learn about life and success from a whole different perspective! A perspective that in the past we have taken for granted and not considered in detail. And yet, when you do consider it in detail, it is a perspective that can make a major difference in your life. What a difference it can and will make when we learn to listen so that others will speak! Listen to win!

INTRODUCTION

Effective listening is a major problem. How many people are willing to admit that failure to listen effectively has had a direct effect on their organization or on them personally? Such an admission borders on the culturally unthinkable. It is easier to point out other people's deficiencies in this area than to admit that we may be part of the problem! In our society, we simply do not know how to listen, we place little value on listening, and there is little information available on the topic.

As important as listening is, you will find little written about it. Occasionally it is buried within another book on management or speaking, but a book that concentrates solely on how to listen so that others will speak is just not available. It is as if this idea is either of secondary importance or of no importance at all. Considering the role that listening plays in organizational and personal effectiveness, this is unbelievable.

If you look at what has happened in business today, and you are aware of the powerful influence of companies in cultures outside of our own, you will realize that major shifts in dominance have occurred and continue to occur. Why is this happening? One very clear and obvious reason is that those in control of companies in cultures outside of our own are listening to their customers. They are listening to their workers. Their workers are listening to their supervisors. And those in control of companies in cultures outside of our own are listening to American companies speak, too. And they are effective, competitive, and successful because of it!

How can American companies win back market share? Is it too late? We think not. But a major change must occur. American managers must do something completely unexpected. They must learn the process of listening. The results of effective listening may not be immediate. But in the long run, the results will become obvious. In the long run, the results will be profound and will show up in the bottom line. In the long run, not only will managers and businesses benefit, but so will workers and the entire American economy. Often such change requires a massive reorientation—beginning with basic building blocks. Such is the case with effective listening.

That is precisely why we begin this book by writing about the need to change habits. That is precisely why we begin by writing about taking charge of your life, because the more control you have, the better listener you are likely to be. That is precisely why we have offered specific intervention strategies designed to help come between you and your habitual ways of behaving. Changing habits requires energy and commitment—a massive reorientation. But this massive reorientation can create positive outcomes: an interesting job, enjoyable relationships, numerous promotions, a higher-quality product, worthwhile contributions to a better world, and a competitive edge in a world marketplace. These are the kinds of changes that will have a lasting, positive effect.

This book touches on the basic and fundamental requirements if change on this scale is to take place. For example, we first discuss the listening process so managers have a firm footing on what the process looks like. Then we examine specifically how managers can listen to improve the work environment, how they can listen so employees will speak, how they can listen so supervisors will speak, how they can find the "trip wires" to increase effectiveness, how they can listen to cope with conflict, how they can listen in meetings, and finally, how they can listen for personal growth.

In short, power-packed chapters, we talk straight from the shoulder. Managers can learn precisely what needs to be done to affect the kind of change that is going to make a difference in the lives of their employees and supervisors, in the life of the business, and in their own personal lives as well. We do not mince words. Managers want information straight, direct, and to the point. That is the kind of information that is most likely to make a difference. That is the kind of information that is most likely to be read. And that is the kind of information most likely to be put into action.

It is, perhaps, an understatement to say that you live in a talk-oriented society. But talk seems to be what it's all about.

That is why we are asking for a massive reorientation. For change to occur you need to stop talking! It is the bottom line of this book. It is the bottom line for effectiveness. It is the bottom line for success. You need to Listen to Win!

PART ONE

WHY DO MANAGERS NEED A BOOK ON LISTENING?

CHAPTER 1

Why Can't You Get Information On Listening?

The phone rang in Mike's office two weeks ago. It was the general manager of the Signature Inn in Columbus, Ohio. He was calling in response to the evaluation card that Mike had filled out two weeks earlier. During his stay at the hotel, he had been rudely treated by a Signature Inn employee. This happened not once, but on three occasions. On the evaluation card, Mike noted the problems that occurred and mentioned his disappointment with the way the problems had been handled at the time.

Randy, the general manager, apologized. He then went on to say that he appreciated Mike taking the time to fill out the evaluation card and that Signature Inn wanted Mike's continued business. Randy also wanted to let Mike know that he was refunding his money and that the employee who had been rude had been disciplined. Four days later, a check arrived in the mail from the Signature Inn Corporation accompanied by a letter of apology from the president of the corporation!

Can you guess which hotel chain Mike stays with when he travels? Listening makes a difference! In a society where people would rather talk than listen, people who listen are not only different, they are several steps ahead. When they listen, they give the organization they represent a positive image as well. The process of listening demonstrates the basic value and importance of customers. It is this value that says in brightly colored, blinking, neon lights, "you are important enough to be listened to." This is what is missing from today's society. People are desperately looking for other people (and organizations) that care about them.

This book on listening came about as the result of an unexpected shopping trip. When we travel we often stop in different parts of the country and look at shopping malls to see what's selling. Inevitably we end up in the bookstores. We had been studying literature on listening, so in between appointments we decided to see what books were available for business people on the subject.

We asked the salesperson to direct us to the section where we could find books on listening. Her quizzical look indicated this was not a typical question. As she searched the aisles, she turned to us and said, "You know, we have lots of books that tell you how to speak so that people will listen, but I don't think we have a single one on how to listen."

As a result of that trip, we began searching other bookstores to see what was available on listening. There are plenty of management books with short subsections on listening. There are also numerous books on speaking that contain small sections on listening. But these books only emphasize how important listening is, and while the authors of these books spend the majority of their time emphasizing this importance, it is as if listening is something that just happens. How to listen so others will speak is secondary, if included at all.

As we continued our search for books on listening, we discovered there is also no shortage of books on quality—the key to good management and customer relations. And while these books often have chapters on managers walking around and rubbing shoulders with customers and coworkers, gaining an appreciation for what they are saying and how they feel, the books treat listening much like the process of osmosis. If managers are there long enough, what customers and coworkers are saying, or how they feel, will simply penetrate by absorption or diffusion—it will soak in through the managers' skins!

Our search did not stop with our discovery of books on good management and customer relations. There were also many books on marketing, or, rather, books emphasizing methods for talking to customers. In marketing, of course, the concept of "listening to customers" is of paramount importance. Focus groups, after all, grew out of marketing. In focus groups, however, the purpose of getting a group of customers to interact does not zero-in on the process of listening. The purpose of focus groups is to have customers tell those in charge the best way to speak—how to present their ideas and their products in the most effective manner.

We found numerous books on marketing, but the authors of these books stressed how to speak loud and clear to customers and how to market yourself to coworkers or to your boss. Once again, listening was absent from their discussion.

Regardless of the discipline, the books we discovered danced around the concept of listening. Somehow, like parents of a disobedient child, authors and leaders in the field do not want to come right out and admit that the problem of ineffective and inefficient listening is partly our own. The idea that poor listening might be a major issue, or that listening is a major reason for failures within organizations, or perhaps that it could be a significant personal problem, borders on the culturally unthinkable. It is easier to point to other people or other concepts rather than come out and admit that in our society we do not place much value on listening. We do not know how to listen effectively. Ours is a society of talk, talk, talk. Listening so people will speak is a concept that is strange, foreign, and bizarre. But that is just what this book is about.

If we had to end this chapter with one important principle for you to carry throughout the book, or if we had to pick just one theme that lies at the heart of all our suggestions, it would be: Listen To Win!

CHAPTER 2

What's In This Book For You?

Now you understand the problem. We don't know how to listen. Second, it seems as if we don't want to learn how to listen. Even if we wanted to learn, books on listening are hard to find. You might be wondering why this is so. While there are many reasons, we'll discuss just two. One may be inherent in the nature or basic characteristics of men and women. Think about men and women you know well. Is it true that men in general tend to talk more and women tend to listen more? At a recent party, we were intrigued at how long Sam, a friend of ours, talked about his job as a journalist and how long Linda, another friend, was willing to listen. Sam was talking in great detail. He was giving detailed information about the operation of his newspaper business and the various departments and divisions. Later, we asked Linda if she was interested in what Sam was saying. Her first response was, "It was interesting." Then she paused and said, "Maybe I found out more than I wanted to know." Still later, Linda confessed to being bored by Sam. Asked why she was willing to listen to him for so long, she said "I'm used to listening to men go on and on. I don't even think about it."

In her best-selling book *You Just Don't Understand: Women and Men in Conversation*, Deborah Tannen explains that this asymmetry (lecturer as teacher/listener as student) occurs because of the differences in men's and women's upbringing. Women tend to build rapport, Tannen suggests, while men value their position at center stage. Women play down their expertise, while men seek opportunities to gather and disseminate factual information. Tannen goes on stating that "typically, men are more comfortable than women in giving information and opinions…whereas women are more comfortable than men in supporting others." The point is that one problem with listening may be inherent in the basic upbringing of men and women.

Another problem may be inherent in our culture. Traditionally listening was seen as a feminine skill (Booth-Butterfield, 1984). Listening is a behavior viewed to be nurturing, compassionate, and even submissive in nature. This type of skill was not seen as important for boys or men to learn. As a result, men manage companies in the same way they have been taught. Dominance and authority was something that came through verbal agility and aggression. Listening was demanded because "I am the boss, and when the boss speaks, you listen!" Being a listener was equated with being subservient to the speaker.

American companies seem to demand that customers listen to them, and bosses and coworkers jockey for the right to be heard. But many companies in cultures outside our own built their existence on effective listening. They listen to customers. Coworkers listen to supervisors. Companies outside of our culture listen to American companies, too. They stake their reputations on effective listening!

A strange thing happened to companies that listened. As they listened, they began to build products that people wanted. With management listening, employees began to talk about how to improve the product. Customers responded to being listened to by buying the products. Suddenly countries that had fewer national resources had companies with results that astonished the world. They tapped a resource that was all but forgotten within American society: the ability to listen and to respond.

It doesn't matter where the problem lies—whether it is the basic nature of men and women or whether it is cultural. Both are likely to be related. But what is important is that we try to solve the problems—lack of concern for the importance of listening, not knowing how to listen, and not wanting to learn about listening.

In the pages that follow, the focus is on learning to do something unexpected: learning the process of listening. This requires that the organization and the individual is committed to a long-range view of organizational and personal growth. Rarely will effective listening give organizations and individuals immediate results, although this sometimes happens. Mike will not go and stay at Signature Inn tonight just to demonstrate his appreciation for the general manager listening to his concerns. But down the road, when he is traveling, his choice will always be the organization that listened to him as a customer.

Mike is just like us, and we are like everyone else—we look for businesses that care and show concern for us as individuals. We want people and organizations that listen to us. Listening is a clear and obvious demonstration of care and concern.

Listening as a means of growth, however, is not for those who need immediate gratification. Rarely will listening give immediate results, but we can assure you that there will be results. These results can have profound, long-term implications for those willing to listen.

What is important to note from this chapter is that although there are differences in the ways men and women respond, and while our culture promotes stereotypes of men being speakers (dominant) and women being listeners (supportive), this does not have to be so. These facts tend to underscore and support our habits. When we recognize that we are responding a certain way because of our sex or because of the way our culture has influenced us, we can change. And change must take place if there is to be organizational and personal growth. This book is about change, and in any program for change, awareness is the first step. What it takes to change our habits is the subject of the next chapter.

CHAPTER 3

What Does It Take To Change Habits?

- Do you tend to squirm and fidget while others are talking?
- Do you brush aside a subordinate's arguments because you are right?
- Are you quick to label a conversation or a speaker as dull or boring?

Although managers face these kinds of situations daily, most would not think of them as problems. But because they respond to situations in a certain way, they miss out on valuable opinions, information, and suggestions. These missed opinions, information, and suggestions may be essential to the company's survival.

The problem with the questions that begin this chapter, and the reason why they are often perceived as problems, is because they are part of our regular way of behaving—our habits. They are behaviors that are embedded from constant use. The task of changing these habits is not easy; however, change is essential.

Better listening behaviors are likely to save time, increase efficiency and productivity, and serve a positive human-relations function. Our success in dealing with these habits is likely to have a direct and measurable effect on others—those with whom we work or those who come into contact with our work. It goes without saying that better methods are likely to have personal benefits. In this chapter, we will answer the question, "What does it take to change habits?"

A habit is something that we do automatically. That is why, first, we seldom recognize things that we do habitually and, second, why we do not label them as problems. Poor listening behaviors are habits, and they are also problems. To change habits requires awareness; that is what this book is all about. But changing habits requires more than that. Some new behaviors—hopefully positive ones—must be put in place of the old behaviors. This is not easy.

In a sense, it requires that the new behavior should be injected between ourselves and the habitual behavior. We must consciously be aware of what we do, and then sensing that what we are doing is negative, weak, destructive, or non-constructive, we must try to do something different. We must have new behaviors (strategies) on hand when needed.

The word *intervention* describes a state of coming between. We will use it here to mean bringing something between us and our habitual behavior. The word strategy means a plan of action. In the military, the word strategy describes the science of planning and directing large-scale military operations—especially maneuvering forces into the most advantageous position prior to actual engagement with the enemy. This isn't so farfetched when dealing with some negative habits! So an intervention strategy involves a plan of action that we can use to put between us and our habitual behavior patterns. To use a military analogy: we want to do battle with the enemy—our weak or nonconstructive habits.

You might be wondering why intervention strategies are important. Gaining peak efficiency often requires changing entrenched habits. Managers, like all business professionals, have been dealing with the problems of poor listening since they were born—and for all of their professional lives. They do not have any ways of dealing with these habits since they are deeply embedded and often are not recognized.

In the book *Interpersonal Communication in Organizations,* authors Baskin and Aronoff write about what happens when we try to introduce new behaviors:

> "The attempt to introduce a new set of behaviors into an organization [or organism] is analogous to the attempt to transplant a new organ into a human being. Even when the new heart or kidney might prolong or save a person's life, the body tries to reject the organ. To the body, which has been genetically programmed to reject foreign cells, the new organ is just another intruder. That process, which

usually protects the organism, in this case may prevent its survival." (Baskin & Aronoff, 1980, p. 137)

Even when the opinions, information, and suggestions we need may be crucial to the survival of an organization, our weak listening habits may be so embedded and resistant to change that we are unable to substitute other behaviors and listen to crucial ideas—or any others' ideas!

Changing habits is not easy. Because we are dealing with entrenched habits, changes that occur are likely to be short-lived, as we revert to former behaviors, patterns, and processes that often are weak or nonconstructive.

The first thing we need to do is to become a self-monitor; become aware of the behaviors we use when we are in listening situations. Doing so will help you answer the following questions:

- Do you choke off an employee's conversation to ask questions? To correct what he or she says? To tell him your views?
- Do you brush aside a subordinate's arguments because you are right?
- Do you frequently have to backtrack because you misunderstood the information or instructions you received?
- Are you quick to label a conversation or a speaker as dull or boring?
- Do you tend to squirm or fidget while others are speaking?
- Do you always know what other people are going to say before they say it?
- Do you listen for other people's feelings, or the emotional content, or for the sense of the message?
- Do you ask people to repeat or ask for a restatement when you haven't heard what they said or are not clear about their meaning?
- Do you think it's all right to only half listen to conversations because you are already forming your answer to what's being said?
- Do you prefer talking to listening?

To change habits, it helps to form an idea as to what an ideal listening situation would be. You will then have a positive, vivid image that will help drive and motivate you to change. When the positive image is as real, specific, and clear as possible, it will have the power, or force, to help you reduce, interrupt, and even ignore external stimuli—the habitual behaviors that control you in listening situations. Whether intervention strategies are going to be effective or not in changing habits depends on the relevance and importance of the sequence of substituted behaviors and their practice.

To make a change of habit possible, three things need to be assured in the construction of the intervention strategy. First, it must be concrete—not general or abstract. The more general and abstract it is, the more the sequence itself will allow for old, negative habits to re-emerge. Second, it must be personalized. Sequences need to be tied directly to personal needs, as well as personal strengths and weaknesses—things we can legitimately do or not do. Sequences suggested by others may work for you, but often they need to be improved or altered to suit your own needs. When personal steps are added or subtracted to make the movement between the steps of the sequence smooth and comfortable, this tailoring ensures that the sequence will be followed. Also, when sequences are personalized, it is easier to imagine each of the steps and our final goal. Finally, sequences must be incremental or systematic. That is, they must provide the specifics to help us get from where we are now to our clear end point or goal.

In constructing sequences throughout this book, we place the final image or goal—in this instance, improved listening—in a cloud. This cloud is used to suggest several things. First, that it is an image to be held in our mind. Second, that it is something to be worked toward—a goal. Third, that it is beyond our grasp at the present time and only through action and problem solving can we attain it. Fourth, the cloud suggests the vividness or the end product—the final image that needs to be carefully, clearly, and realistically created so that it can be controlled and kept in mind.

There is another advantage of having a clearly constructed sequence and final goal. Both allow us to cue or prompt appropriate behavior. Because we are dealing with habits, we need cues or prompts to intervene that will trigger us to remember what we are supposed to do. For example, when we drink orange juice in the morning it can prompt us to take our pills. When the alarm goes off, it prompts a sequence of exercise routines we engage in. If the intervention strategy is vivid and clear, and if it has a well-defined final goal, it also will serve as a cue or will prompt a desired action.

You might wonder what it is that motivates us to move from one step to another up the intervention strategy ladder. That is, what is it that makes us want to implement it? There are numerous motivators. The first may be the most important: self-image improvement. When we are more effective and efficient, for example a better listener, we feel better about ourselves. Because our success has a direct effect on others, and others influence our own self-image, this will be an additional, increased, and reinforcing benefit to our self-concept. It may result in better interpersonal relations, a better work and home environment, greater happiness, better health, more money, and greater success. It could cause us to respond in direct and meaningful ways to situations that could be hazardous or catastrophic.

Listening Effectively

We will offer an intervention strategy here for improved listening. Be aware that parts of it may need altering to make it more succinct, more beneficial, or more personal for you. For example, some situations do not call for "making notes," so step six could be dropped. Basically, this is what improved listening requires:

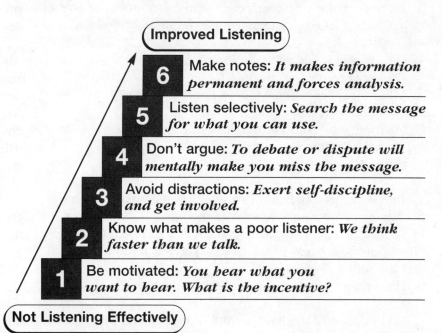

Improved Listening

6 Make notes: *It makes information permanent and forces analysis.*

5 Listen selectively: *Search the message for what you can use.*

4 Don't argue: *To debate or dispute will mentally make you miss the message.*

3 Avoid distractions: *Exert self-discipline, and get involved.*

2 Know what makes a poor listener: *We think faster than we talk.*

1 Be motivated: *You hear what you want to hear. What is the incentive?*

Not Listening Effectively

Not Listening Effectively

Most intervention strategies need alteration. A single sequence is unlikely to be perfect for everyone. Any one of the steps above could be expanded to become a full sequence. What does it take, for example, to be motivated? Poor listening may be caused by different things in different people:

- tuning out
- weak attention span
- poor evaluation or analysis skills
- inability to assess facts or detect weaknesses
- limited physical (hearing) skills

Also, there are likely to be any number of potential distractions that require control. How does one prevent the desire to argue in people who are prone to argument? Or how can people listen selectively? What are the keys to effective note-taking? The point, we think, is clear. We cannot assume that everyone is at the same stage or place in their lives when it comes to adopting or using intervention strategies. That is why *personalizing* our strategies is important.

To answer the question posed at the beginning of this chapter, "What does it take to change habits?" requires several responses:

(1) awareness and self-monitoring,
(2) a positive mental attitude,
(3) some specific behaviors to put in place
    of the negative habits,
(4) some motivation or desire to engage in the
    specific behaviors, and
(5) practice.

Habits are not changed overnight. Remember, they have been in place for almost as long as you have. It may take time to change them. Do not give up. Stick to it. When it comes to effectiveness, success in many managerial activities depends on how well you listen.

How can you change a poor listening habit?

(1) Recognize that you are not unique. Don't put yourself down for not listening well. Almost everyone suffers

from ineffective listening at one time or another; some suffer from it much of the time. Recognize that something can be done about it. It does not have to be a lifetime handicap.

(2) Fully admit, up front, that you do not listen as well as you want to.

(3) Take responsibility for your poor listening. You don't need to collapse into guilt or launch into self-flagellation. Just acknowledge that your poor listening is in some way caused by you.

(4) Look closely within. Look beyond the problem of poor listening. Get in touch with your feelings. Get in touch with the benefits that can come from effective listening. Get in touch with what you can do to prepare the way—thoughts, feelings, and action—so that the proper context or foundation for effective listening is established.

(5) Begin to prepare for listening situations. Think about the intervention strategy we proposed above. Begin to practice it on your own so that you become familiar with the steps. Prepare for communication situations as a listener just as carefully and thoughtfully as you prepare to communicate with others.

(6) Plan ahead. Know what you are going to do. Believe that there is something that you can gain by listening in every communication situation.

(7) Look at listening experiences as adventures and opportunities for learning and growth. Focus on the pleasures of listening to other people and of complimenting them with your interest and attention.

(8) Smile and look confident, even if you don't feel it. Try to project sincerity, empathy, and compassion.

Remember, habits can be changed. It is up to us to change. Changing habits takes time and effort, but when the bad habit is poor listening, the payoff is in more and better information and the benefit is in substantial learning. Most important, the benefit is in better human relations.

CHAPTER 4

Where Can You Begin?

What we discuss in this chapter may be the most radical of all the ideas presented in this book, particularly if you have never heard of it or do not believe it. *The extent to which you are in charge of your life determines how successful you are in life.* This means that you are in charge of your own success, and this is directly related to effective listening. The more *control* you have, the better listener you are likely to be. In this chapter we examine internal versus external control and why change in your outlook on this concept is important. More importantly, we discuss *how* you can gain internal control—where can you begin? Finally, we look at taking charge of your life and what it means.

WHAT ARE WE TALKING ABOUT?

The first term that is important to grasp is "locus" or "place of control," which means belief or non-belief in our ability to influence our lives. *Locus of control* scales divide people into two groups. The "internals" are those who believe in their ability to exercise control over their lives or control their own destiny. Internals act as though what is going on within them affects what is going on outside them. Internally oriented people believe they are creators of their experiences.

The second group in which locus of control scales divide people is "externals." Externals believe their lives are controlled by forces outside themselves, such as luck, fate, or powerful others. Externals perceive themselves as victims of circumstance and would think or say the following: "I couldn't do it because there wasn't enough time, the directions were unclear, or the proper materials were not supplied." (Insert your own excuse.) Externals operate at the effect of conditions outside of themselves.

WHY IS CHANGE IMPORTANT?

You might wonder why changing from an external to an internal perspective is important. At first, if you think of these two concepts based on the definitions offered earlier you might see being an external as superior. Why take responsibility for your life if you don't need to? Most people feel things are all right the way they are. Why change? As Illinois State University President Dr. Thomas Wallace once said, "The only people who desire change are babies with dirty diapers."

Internal control—taking charge of your life—is essential to both positive self-esteem and good psychological health. Education research has shown that people who have greater internal control score higher on achievement tests, get better grades, and display superiority in acquiring and using information. Why do internals do so well? Because they *think* they are in charge of their lives, they strive to achieve more, they attempt to perform better, and they make better use of the information they receive.

Internals do better in life as well. Let's look at some of the research results concerning motivators to change. Internals reveal:

- better skill in dealing with conformity situations
- more willingness to engage in risk-taking
  (growth experiences)
- greater desire for skill-oriented rewards
- higher levels of aspiration
- greater tendencies to forget failures
- stronger attempts to control the environment
- clearer resistance to subtle suggestion
- more assertiveness
- more ambition and industriousness.

These characteristics present exciting prospects for growth, development, and change in our lives. How can we get a better handle on our lives? Fortunately people can shift from external to internal controls. Research indicates that even a slight shift toward a more internal orientation can be beneficial. Locus of control is modifiable; we can gain greater control.

WHERE CAN YOU BEGIN?

Any successful program for personal change has four elements. First, people must be aware of situations or motives. Second, there must be self-study in relation to that situation or motive. Third, there must be planning or goal setting. And finally, there must be energy or commitment to the plan. Let's apply these four elements to a concrete situation. You have an important project due, but numerous distractions occur to keep you from completing the project. Here is a simple situation in which greater control may be exerted. How can you change?

First, you need to be aware of the situation. Let's suppose that your normal, habitual response is to allow yourself to be distracted—to answer the phone, to respond to colleagues, to finish memos, or to answer the mail.

Second, you need to do some self-study in relation to the situation. For example, you need to ask, "What would work best for me?" Nobody else can answer this question for you. Let's say, for example, that this project might lead to a promotion, a favorable review by a superior, or better recognition for your department or team. There is no doubt that you are going to resist distractions to get the results that occur from completing the project.

The third element is planning or goal-setting. This is where an intervention strategy like the one introduced in Chapter 3 becomes useful. We need to define priorities, exert self-discipline, and find some structure that we can rely on rather than our habitual response—which is to respond to the distractions. We need a specific, well-planned, clear-cut plan of action.

The following intervention strategy addresses the situation above. However, it is important to note that what we propose here is just one possible intervention strategy. Your strategy may be personalized to meet your specific, individual situation.

Greater Self-Discipline

4 Be decisive: *"I'll have to contact you tomorrow after I finish a project."*

3 Respond gently: *"I appreciate your call; thank you for your concern and interest."*

2 Count to Ten (relax): *Provide a suggestion, "I want to stay focused and complete the project."*

1 Awareness of the Situation: *"I want more control of my life in these situations."*

Not Enough Self-Discipline

Not Enough Self-Discipline

Step two—count to 10 and relax—is important. To change habits requires intervention. To make change possible, we need to relax. Only in a relaxed state are we able to accept positive suggestions. A "suggestion" simply may be an internal message, such as, "I want to be more energetic," "I want to be more assertive," "I want to be decisive," "I want to be able to cope effectively with problems," "I want to be more self-confident," or "I want to be less dependent on external events"—whatever direction you want to see change.

The fourth step involves energy or commitment to your plan. An important factor is the plan's realism. Is it practical and realistic? Can you actually do it? Another factor is your reward for completing the plan. Rewards cannot always be predicted; some are short-range and some are long-range rewards. The point is, if the goal is significant, relevant, and achievable, then it can be approached and accomplished. This only can be determined by the person who has constructed the plan.

TAKE CHARGE OF YOUR LIFE!

The way we act reflects our choices. All of our choices have resulted in where we are in life. It is these same choices that create the habits—good and bad—that guide many of our actions. While our behaviors are often subtle, based on decisions that occur at the rate of thousands per hour, we are not always conscious of how our choices have led us to our current situation. This is precisely how habits form—without awareness.

But the "take charge of your life" philosophy allows us to take a look at how we create our experiences through our thoughts and choices. It forces us to:

1. Recognize that we create our experiences. Effective listening is our problem.
2. Accept total responsibility for our experiences. If we realize we are responsible for what happens in our lives, then we are responsible for any change that may occur. To be a better listener means we need to act.
3. Become aware of the alternatives available to us for improvement and change. With the power to take charge of our experiences, we are more inclined to look for opportunities.

Why not? Our experiences have a direct effect on our life; we do have control.

SUMMARY

Being an internal person puts the responsibility in our hands. This chapter showed you how you can help create a positive attitude. Using an "internal focus" throughout this book will help you to examine in greater detail, understand the discussion, and apply the material to your own life. Internally oriented people take charge of their lives. What would you have done in a certain situation? What could you have done better? So, to answer the question "Where Can You Begin?" the answer is clear. Begin by adopting an "internal" mentality. Begin by taking charge of your life. Striving to be internally oriented makes us conscious of our choices and our thoughts. It creates positive outcomes: an interesting job, enjoyable relationships, numerous promotions, and worthwhile contributions to a better world. When we take charge of our lives we ask, "How did we choose to be a poor listener?" We also ask, "How can we become a more effective listener?" To do so we need a plan of action. We need to exert energy and make a commitment to the plan. We know that if we gain greater control of our lives, we become more effective listeners. Let's apply the above intervention strategy to a situation where we need to listen for information:

1. Be aware of the situation. ("I am not listening well.")
2. Provide a direct suggestion. ("I want to be an effective listener in this situation.")
3. Respond gently; remain calm. ("I appreciate your concern [use when addressing a person who is distracting you], and thank you for sharing with me.")
4. Be decisive. ("I need this information right now" [while pointing to the person to whom you need to listen] and "I will have to address your concerns later" [directed to the person who is distracting you].)

Listen to win!

PART TWO

WHAT DO MANAGERS NEED TO KNOW ABOUT THE LISTENING PROCESS?

CHAPTER 5

What Does Listening Require You To Do?

Michelle was thoroughly frustrated. The materials she had instructed Loren, her manager, to have in place for the upcoming seminar were nowhere to be seen. When Michelle confronted Loren with the problem, his response was, "I didn't hear you tell me that you wanted them." Michelle knew that she told him, so either he wasn't listening or he just didn't hear her.

Listening is not just hearing. Listening is more than simply an exercise in hearing sounds that surround us on a daily basis. Often we hear people without listening to them. For example, how many times have you listened to a speaker, absorbing the content, when suddenly you realize you are just hearing the words while off in your own thoughts and images? Or how often have you been receiving complicated instructions and understanding them, but when you get one that you can't understand, all of the rest of the instructions become jumbled noises?

If listening were merely translating sounds into meaning, how could we explain the fact that people without hearing can listen? Listening is a process; it is a learned process. Different cultures and different people learn to listen in different ways.

According to a study by Baker and Morgan (1985), people in the United States spend 80% of their lives communicating. Of this 80%, 16% is spent reading, 9% is spent writing, 30% represents speaking, and 45% is spent listening. *(See Figure 5.1.)* From birth to death, we do more listening than any other form of communicating. Yet how often do we actually stop and think about how important it is to lis-

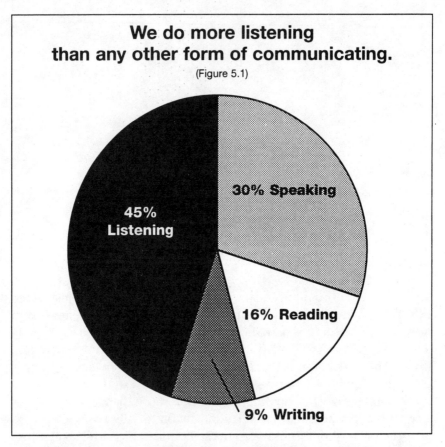

**We do more listening
than any other form of communicating.**
(Figure 5.1)

30% Speaking

45%
Listening

16% Reading

9% Writing

ten? How often do we think about what it really means to listen? We take the process for granted.

If you are typical, this is the point where you may be tempted to skip the technical stuff and go on to what you see as "the real stuff"—the practical application. Theory isn't nearly as important as how to apply that theory. "Cut to the chase," someone might say. "I don't need all of that theory bunk. I want to know the suggestions for making it make a difference in my life." If these are your feelings, feel free to speed-read through this section or even skip over it for now, but plan to come back to it because it gives an important and useful framework for further application. The material that follows this chapter will make more sense if you first understand the theory behind it. Most people do not know, nor do they want to understand, the basics behind effective listening.

If your goal is to be an effective listener, then you will want to get as much out of the process as possible. To get the most from this book, you must understand theory to make the use and application more meaningful. Remember, knowledge meets wisdom at the point of application. This simply means that you cannot get wise by skipping over the knowledge—the basics. So speed through it now if you wish, but plan to come back to it and read it carefully. Understanding the theory will help make effective listening easier, more pleasurable, and more rewarding.

Let's return to the difference between hearing and listening. Some readers may think that we are playing a word game and that there is no real difference at all. Hearing is a physical process that we do with our ears. Hearing is also one of our five senses, along with seeing, smelling, tasting, and touching. Notice that when the senses are listed, listening is never one of them. One way to remember this is to remember the aphorism coined by Frank Tyger, "Hearing is one of the body's five senses. But listening is an art."

Because hearing is a physical process that we do with our ears alone, unless we are physically impaired, we can hear. The process of hearing involves sound waves hitting our eardrums. Picture this: Bryan is sitting with a group of employees listening to the boss talk about a future project. Bryan can hardly stay awake. Suddenly the boss looks at him and says "Bryan?" Bryan perks up and says, "I'm listening." The boss says, "Good, we need you on board for this project."

Technically, Bryan was wrong. He was hearing, *not* listening. Sound waves were hitting his ear drums, but little else was happening. What is it that makes listening different from this physical activity?

Listening is a three-part process that includes hearing, thinking, and feeling. Listening includes hearing, but hearing does not include listening. In other words, listening includes the physical, mental, and emotional. If people's thoughts and emotions are not engaged (active), if they are not thinking and feeling, then they are not listening, they are only hearing. Hearing requires no thought and no feeling. That is why Bryan was wrong. Sound waves were hitting his ear drums, but because he was barely able to stay awake, his thinking and feeling processes were inhibited or totally unengaged (nonactive).

Why is it important to remember the difference between hearing and listening? Because if we are to listen, we must try to make certain that we are in a position—ready and able—to think and feel. When we are drowsy, lazy, inattentive, or bored, we are not likely to be able to listen, at least not at our full potential. Even when we can't concentrate, for example, when our own thoughts and feelings are interfering, we are not going to listen well.

Thinking and feeling go on in our heads. This means that if we want to listen effectively, we must prepare mentally first, even if only momentarily. It is that moment of mental preparation that allows us to concentrate and understand. And that is precisely what separates hearing from listening. If our minds are truly engaged on the other person and his or her ideas, we are listening. If not, we are merely hearing. Listening, then, is like capitalizing on the hearing process. It means taking it two steps further. And these two steps are what makes a difference in effectiveness. What does listening require that you do? Go the extra mile? No. Just two steps: thinking and feeling.

CHAPTER 6

Why Must You Understand The Process Of Reduction?

When Art, an advertising department manager, listened to a presentation for a new product launch, he thought he was listening to the entire presentation by the new product division manager. At the celebration of the new product launch, he was asked several questions about the project. Unable to remember details, Art asked someone else for some of the answers. But when Art was asked questions about anything that had to do with the advertising of the product, his memory was not only accurate, he also could remember details and precise facts.

What Art did in the above instance was reduce the amount of information to a manageable level—that which pertained to him and his department. This type of reduction is sometimes referred to as *selective attention,* reducing the amount of information we must process at any one time.

As we learned in Chapter 5, the process of listening begins with hearing. We then perceive incoming information through our senses. The process then moves to our assessment and application of that information and ends with our action or reaction to what we have perceived. *(See Figure 6.1.)* Listening can be thought of as a "process of reduction."

From the moment we get up in the morning to the moment we go to bed at night, we are perceiving the world around us. But we are also taking what we perceive and reducing it to a manageable size. How does this process of reduction occur? Stop reading right now. Look around you and listen. All of the sounds you now hear, all of the

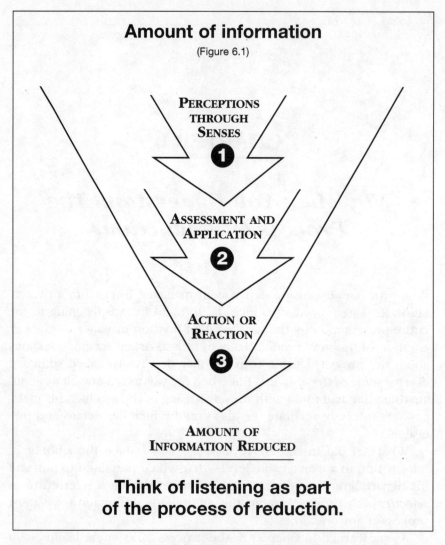

Amount of information

(Figure 6.1)

PERCEPTIONS
THROUGH
SENSES
❶

ASSESSMENT AND
APPLICATION
❷

ACTION OR
REACTION
❸

AMOUNT OF
INFORMATION REDUCED

**Think of listening as part
of the process of reduction.**

things that you now see, and everything that you sense existed before this moment. But you chose to focus on reading and the images generated by these words, rather than hearing, seeing, and sensing things not related to these words. This is the process of reduction.

Reduction is a critical concept to understand. To listen effectively and to give feedback appropriately we have to acknowledge and compensate for the fact that we are reducing parts of the world and the information that keeps coming at us. We do this to keep our lives manageable, to make sense of the blooming, buzzing, confusion of life. We do this to keep ourselves sane.

Look at Figure 6.1 again. We begin life with exposure to certain parts of the world. By where we live, by what jobs we hold, and by who our families are, we construct reduction mechanisms that limit the flow of information we receive about the world. Just by living in the U.S., for example, and not traveling abroad, it is difficult to understand the tremendous number of choices we are faced with daily. No other country in the world has supermarkets lined with the number of products available in the U.S. But when we shop in a supermarket, we make selections similar to those made the last time we shopped. Our reduction mechanism restricts our choices to the familiar brands to which we have become accustomed or been exposed to through television advertising. In other countries, shoppers do not have the same elaborate reduction mechanisms in place for supermarket shopping; they don't need to—there are far fewer choices available to them.

Our jobs help form our reduction mechanisms as well. Just notice how carefully we listen when our employer talks about cutbacks to see if our job, our department, or our division will be affected. Notice how different people describe a car accident based on their job. An engineer might describe the structural damage based on the plan, design, and construction of the car. A doctor might describe the damage done to the occupants of the automobile. A lawyer might see the accident from the angle of potential litigation and fault. Each of these people has reduced the amount of information available just as Art did in the beginning of this chapter.

Even our families and the way we are raised can affect our reducing mechanisms. Families tend to instill values. Whatever these values are, we tend to gather information that reinforces and buttresses those values. We reduce all that we see and hear to those things that align with our values. Often we seek out only the information which supports our values. "Limited exposure" is an immediate reduction of the information available. Families serve as a reduction influence whether children follow in their parents' footsteps or choose different sandals. Why is it, for example, that so many sons and daughters go on in life to do the same kinds of things that their parents did? Because it is those things that reaffirm the values instilled in them as children. Children feel most comfortable with those same values. And it is by doing things that support those values that tends to bring happiness and continued success.

In addition to where we live, the jobs we have, and the families we grew up in, people often have biases and prejudices about things they have never seen, people they have never met, and experiences they have never had. The reason for this is that the world in which they grew up and the world in which they now live reduces their perspectives and exposure. Think of parents who are prejudiced against individuals of another race. Chances are strong that their children will grow up reflecting these same prejudices. Why? Because the family reduced the children's exposure to information. The family effectively places hidden filters on their children, filters that reduce the information flow. Only when these filters are recognized can they be removed.

As we noted, "hidden filters" can also be placed on us as a result of where we live, the jobs we have, or the families we grow up in. But these hidden filters can also result from religion, friends, movies, television, fantasies, experiences, travel, and any number of sources. The importance of filters is discussed in the next chapter.

When we act or react with respect to our perceptions, we take the last step in the reduction process. This reduction takes place in our action or reaction, when we give verbal and nonverbal feedback to people we talk to. How many times after talking with someone do you think to yourself, "That wasn't what I meant to say" or "Why didn't I say what I was thinking?" You are experiencing the reduction that occurs in the action and reaction stage.

Public speakers experiencing stage fright often demonstrate the following: They get up to speak, but their nervousness prevents them from acting or reacting in the way they know they should or in the way they planned to. They are experiencing an "internal reduction" that occurs in the action and reaction stage. We may not be aware of this stage because it can be a reduction that changes our behavior due to an uncontrollable response—in this instance nerves.

The world in which we live exposes us to new information, new ideas, and a steady stream of "sensual data"—information that reaches our senses. Since our perceptions take in information on a continuing basis, reduction is automatic. We can't see everything in a supermarket; we can't listen to every conversation at a party; and we can't take in all the stimulation that may be available at a concert. Seldom can we take in everything one person says to us. Our perception helps us screen out what is not important at a given moment. When you stop reading this book and you allow your senses to become aware of all the things going on around you, you allow your senses to give you different kinds of information. Throughout our lives, the brain channels and reduces the information that is received to make it manageable.

In developing good listening skills, the more we understand and recognize the reduction process that occurs in our own behavior during the three phases of listening, the more likely we will be able to change with the situation. Reduction is positive when it allows us to be focused; it is negative when it prevents us from getting the whole picture. Never assume that you have every piece of information in the listening process—you don't. But don't hesitate to use every piece of information that you have to make good decisions and listen more effectively.

The more we understand reduction, the more we understand how much we do not know, the more tolerant we become of others' information and ideas, and the more we realize the need for more information. The more we understand reduction, the more patient we become, because it is through patience that we wait for more information. The more we understand reduction, the better listeners we become.

CHAPTER 7

What Happens When Information Is Sent Through Filters?

Have you ever received a piece of information and twisted it to conform to what you think is being said? For example, you thought a report is due at the end of the week. Today is Tuesday, but your supervisor drops by your office and tells you he wants the report tonight. What you hear, because you know the report is due Friday, is not tonight, but Thursday. You do not finish the report on time because you did not really listen to your supervisor.

The process of reduction shown briefly in Figure 6.1 does not end with the processes displayed there. As we deal with information at each of the three major stages of reduction, we reduce it further by sending it through filters. Sometimes, as in the opening example, we are not aware of the filter operating. In that example, the filter is really our expectations; we expected to hear what we thought to be correct. That was how the word "tonight" became "Thursday" for you. "The report should not cover," could be heard "The report should cover," or "It should be delivered by mail," could be heard "It should be delivered to Mel." So often, we hear what we expect to hear, what we want to hear, or what our filters cause us to hear.

Our experiences are often the first filter. *(See Figure 7.1.)* How our experiences apply to the situation is the second filter. The third filter often is our own egoism—our ongoing desire to know, "What's in this for me?" If all of the reports we have prepared before covered a brief history of the situation being reported on, then we might hear a direction that said, "The report should not cover history," to say, "The report should cover history."

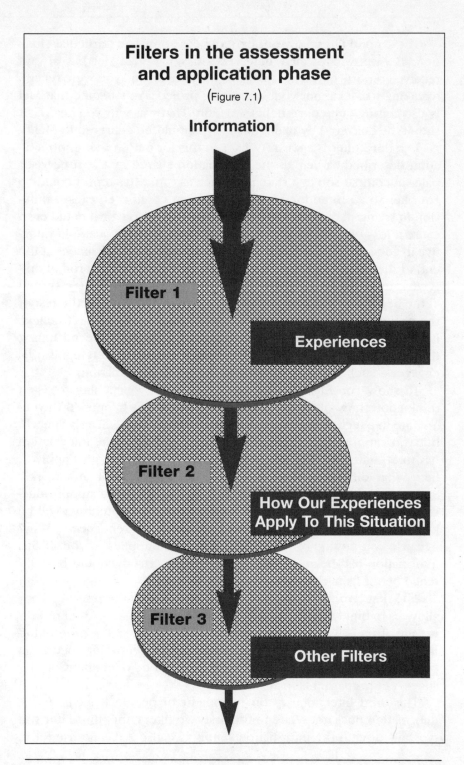

Filters in the assessment and application phase

(Figure 7.1)

Information

Filter 1

Experiences

Filter 2

How Our Experiences Apply To This Situation

Filter 3

Other Filters

The second filter, how our experiences apply to a particular situation, is briefly explained here. Let's assume that Mel has always received reports of the kind you are working on and you were recently talking to Mel about your upcoming project. You assume that Mel is also getting the report in this situation. That was why you heard, "It should be delivered by mail," to say, "It should be delivered to Mel."

The third filter is egoism. What's in this for me? In the report situation described earlier, all the information shared by the supervisor pales in comparison to a statement such as, "And this report could be your key to a promotion." Such a statement could even cause confusion in trying to capture all of the other information, or it could even cause a loss of some of the other information. There is an old directive in education that suggests teachers should pass back grades at the end of the hour. "And this report could be your key to a promotion," is close to saying, "You received an 'A.' " When an 'A' paper is returned at the beginning of a period, the student finds listening for the rest of the period difficult, if not impossible. Thoughts like "I can't believe it," or "I am so good!" or "I can't wait to tell my friends," keep running through the student's mind. The same occurs when egoism is engaged—such as it may have been in this report situation.

To show you how egoism gets involved in your ability to listen think about how often the following example has happened to you. You are in a technical lecture, listening to an expert deliver a speech, but you cannot, for the life of you, figure out what the information has to do with you. You might be thinking, "How does this apply to me? What difference does this make in my life or in my work?" Suddenly, the speaker says, "The ideas and vocabulary I am introducing here will affect all of you because of the new system we will be introducing." Just as quickly, your attention is enhanced. Why? Because you now know how the information applies to you. If this information had been introduced first, you certainly would have listened better from the start.

The first two filters interconnect the past with the present. They allow us to build on the past, using the information for greater or lesser gain. This is why the more experiences we have, the more information and ideas we have to apply to the present. Our success in preparing the report, for example, is likely to be dependent on our success in preparing all prior reports.

The third filter focuses on fulfillment of personal needs. If the information does not relate to the first two filters, the third filter will typically discard the information simply because it has no use for it.

This third filter demands that something be related to me. If there is no common ground, it is hard to figure out how the information relates, and it will be difficult to listen to what is being said, as in the example of listening to the speaker above.

While these are three broad filters, many smaller filters also exist. Some of these smaller filters were referred to in the last chapter. The type of day that we are having can become a filter to our listening ability. If we had a fight with our spouse or significant other, this also becomes a filter to our next encounter. Expectations can be filters as in the opening example. Some filters are short-lived; others are not.

An example of a short-lived filter often occurs in Stan. Stan is a writer, but he is also a business executive. Often when he has insomnia, he gets up and writes late at night. This reduces his ability to think as creatively and listen as effectively the following day. When he gets up the next morning, he acknowledges this filter (lack of sleep) and he reminds himself not to make hasty decisions that day.

Filters created by the reduction of information such as sexism, racism, or ageism may be strongly ingrained and not as easy to identify, acknowledge, or compensate for. Lack of sleep is an easy filter to control. All filters play a role in reducing the information that we are able to use for decision making, creative problem solving, and personal growth. Because they inhibit and restrict information, filters also inhibit and restrict us in a wide variety of ways.

The most effective listening comes when we acknowledge the reduction and filtering processes. With acknowledgment we become more flexible in our responses to the processes, and we learn how to control our responses. Let's look at the following example. We know that Lou does not like one of his colleagues. When we found out the colleague was female, we asked Lou about his feelings about working with females. He said that it didn't matter to him if he worked with males or females. However, later when Lou received information from Sandra, he told us he was aware of his feelings. He made a stronger effort to listen and to respond appropriately just because he was asked earlier about his feelings about working with females. Later, he admitted that before we had asked him about his feelings he did treat the information he received from Sandra as less important or less reliable. When Lou faced and acknowledged this filter, he improved his listening—especially to female coworkers.

While reduction is automatic, filtering is not. Reduction is not negative unless we are unable to acknowledge that it is taking place. Filtering becomes negative when we are unable to recognize and change dysfunctional filters to meet the process of changing demands. With women more prominent in the work force, it was clearly time for Lou to face the seriousness of his filter.

The most effective listeners are those who recognize the filtering process while it is happening and can adapt to meet the needs of those they are encountering.

We end this chapter with a short quiz on your filters. The important question is, "Are my filters clouding my vision and decision-making ability?" To find out the impact of your filters on your vision and decision-making ability, answer each of the following questions first. Do this before reading the information we have added after each question in parentheses.

1. Are my decisions based on a gut reaction, or are they based on objective facts? (If they're based on gut reaction, it's likely numerous filters are intervening in the decisions. Gut reactions tend to be emotional reactions.)

2. What emotions are your decisions evoking? (When decisions are based on objective facts, there is less emotional involvement. When emotions are evoked, it is likely that filters are operating.)

3. What is your first response tendency? (Your first response tendency will most likely demonstrate which filter is dictating your judgment. Our first response tendency is similar to a gut reaction. Getting beyond the first response tendency and the gut reaction requires acknowledgment, patience, and work.)

4. What experiences does this immediately call to mind? (When filters are operating, when the filters are pronounced, and when we are unaware of them, it is likely that they may be stereotypical, prejudicial, biased, racial, sexist, ageist, or something else. Filters can seriously cloud how we obtain information, how much information we gain, and how objective the information we get is.)

To answer the question, "What happens when your information is sent through filters?" the answer is clear. The information is deformed, contorted, misshapen, warped, bent, curved, and twisted. The information does not accurately reflect reality. It cannot be trusted or used by itself for decision-making, problem-solving, or positive personal growth. To know that this process of filtering is occurring and how seriously it occurs can help us acknowledge it, compensate for it, respond to it, and deal with it appropriately. That is what effective listening is all about—flexibility.

CHAPTER 8

How Do The Three Phases Of The Listening Process Affect You?

Anthony was part of a car pool of five men who lived in the same community and traveled to work together every workday. All were eager talkers. When Anthony was traveling to work one day, talking in the back seat of the car with Steve about a movie he saw recently, he overheard Fred talking in the front seat. Actually, what caught his attention was the word "Susan." Anthony was single and had been interested in Susan since he met her several months ago at a company picnic. What was interesting was that Anthony could block out Steve's whole conversation and listen to Fred talk about Susan.

Let's go back to the perception stage. *(See Figure 6.1.)* Perception is not limited to simply hearing the sounds of those who are speaking to us, as Anthony was doing to Steve. Perception takes place primarily in two ways: first, it occurs when we hear the sounds and sense nonverbal communication. Second, it occurs when we selectively choose to acknowledge and attend to a select group of these perceptions, like what Fred was saying about Susan. We cannot acknowledge every piece of information that we receive from our senses, so we selectively choose certain perceptions and give our attention to them.

Sitting in a crowded diner we may ignore the crowds of people talking to give our attention to a juicy story a friend is telling about a coworker. But when we realize that we have heard it before, we find our senses acknowledging the conversation from the next table over as we seem to suddenly hear them talking about a recent news event.

Here is another example: A boss is talking to her secretary. The secretary begins the process of listening before hearing the words.

She begins by observing nonverbal behavior. Is her boss smiling? Is she frowning? What do her eyes say about what she is saying? The secretary is perceiving what she senses and what she hears. Does this mean those are the only perceptions that are coming to her at this moment? Hardly. But she is choosing to reduce the information she perceives in order to pick up what she feels is most valuable. Choosing to reduce information is a natural, normal process. *It is what you choose to focus on that is critical!* Choice is the key element here.

Think for a moment about a job interview. During interviews, all our perceptions are at work as we interact with applicants. Many things affect our impression of applicants—how they look and how they smell. Don't kid yourself, how people smell affects how you listen to them. How people act, how far they stand from you, how they shake hands, how they answer questions during the interview, as well as other factors, all make an impression. These same impressions are at work in the perception process of listening.

We begin selectively perceiving what is being said long before people open their mouth. What's more, the people who are successful in their jobs are the ones who have learned to focus their perceptions beyond what comes to them easily in the natural reduction process. It is easy, for example, to focus on the words alone. Or it is easy to let stereotypes, prejudices, biases, and our emotions, guide our reactions. *It is easy to go with the flow.* What we have to do is control these natural, initial responses. To go beyond these first responses takes awareness, patience, and effort.

The next phase in the listening process is the assessment and application of these perceptions to our lives. People are egocentric and selective beings. We all want to know how it applies to "us," and we want to hear what confirms "our" own desires. Have you ever sat in a meeting and asked yourself, "What's in this for me? What am I supposed to get out of this?" That's egoism, or egocentrism, as some people define it.

The stage of listening most important to understanding the content of what is being said occurs in the assessment and application of your perceptions. In the perception stage discussed earlier we pushed ourselves to broaden our choices by gaining more information. In the assessment stage we challenge ourselves to broaden the application process.

From the first moment we encounter someone, we assess and apply our perceptions of their verbal and nonverbal behaviors

— through the reducing filters of our own life experience. Anthony's first impression of Susan at the company picnic is a good example. Like a prism reflecting sunlight, what we perceive in our mind is suddenly reflected through a vast array of differing experiences. Anthony's past experiences with women will likely affect his reaction to Susan. Our responses are colored in ways other people may or may not have intended. Consequently the content is translated into what we understand through our past. The ability to withhold the mental responses we immediately feel is almost impossible. But the ability to recognize and move beyond these immediate responses is critical to effective content assessment and application. We must be flexible to fully benefit from potentially valuable information.

If Anthony was talking to Susan, for example, it would be easy for him to let his emotions and his attraction to her affect all his perceptions. But what if he heard that she was much older than him or was a different religion or political persuasion? What if she was from a different country, had a different educational level, or preferred different interests, sports, and hobbies? What if she was seriously involved with another person? Would he still overlook all these differences because of his emotions and his attraction? If so, what could be said with some assurance is that Anthony is being inflexible and would benefit from this valuable information.

One reason that many of our first impressions of others—like Anthony's first impression of Susan at the company picnic—are inaccurate is because our emotions intrude on our good judgment. We are *not* saying Susan is not right for Anthony, we are saying that Anthony's first reaction is not based on solid, objective information. His first impression is based on his emotions and his physical attraction to her. During the infatuation stage of courtship, a similar situation to first impressions occurs. Our unreasoning passion or attraction colors our perceptions and decisions, and our perceptions cannot be trusted.

The point here is not to dismiss first impressions nor to dismiss the importance of infatuation, it is to encourage awareness, first, and the need for flexibility, second. When information is important, such as when we are involved in the process of making major decisions or solving significant problems, we need to recognize how and why information is being reduced.

Remaining flexible is especially important as we take what we perceive and attach meaning to it. When we listen to language, we are attaching societal meaning to sounds. This also occurs when we attach common meaning to the nonverbal behavior that we encounter. Remember asking for your first date? As your heart pound-ed and as the adrenaline rushed, your eyes were straining for clues to what she was thinking as your ears were begging to hear her reply. How she responded made the difference in how you felt. You were eagerly engaged in attaching meaning to both the sounds and to the other information coming through your senses. Our perceptions are always attaching meaning to the stimuli that we encounter. It is at this point where listening begins.

In recognizing that we live in a global village, it is important to realize that attaching societal meaning to verbal and nonverbal com-munication is a process of reduction. In a global economy, cross-cul-tural communication is essential. One of the reasons Americans have difficulty communicating cross-culturally is a reluctance to recognize this form of reduction. Our nonverbal communication and our lan-guage are ways that we reduce the information to make it usable. Other cultures also use this reduction process, but they use it in dif-ferent ways.

When we, as Americans, communicate cross-culturally we hesitate to give up our meanings within the communication process. We want other cultures to broaden their perspective to suit us and to include ours. We want them to change their assessments and applications in communicating with us. When we use an incorrect gesture, such as President George Bush revealing the back of his hand when he was in Australia, we think nothing of it; seldom, if ever, apologize; and, often think, "How could they possibly think *that* is offensive?"

The hesitancy to learn how to communicate cross-culturally is an ethnocentric approach to the societal reduction of information. It is that feeling that our nation, our race, and our culture is superior to all others. And because of this feeling, we limit our flexibility. How can we, for example, communicate effectively with people from another culture who believe that the time they show up for an appointment is not important? This is especially the case when we feel that when people show up late, it is an affront and a serious breach of proper etiquette. To be effective in other cultures, we must begin by broad-ening the reduction process at this stage, the stage of the assessment and application of meaning.

The assessment and application of meaning stage is an important one. When Evan, one of our friends, first saw Linda in college, he immediately wanted to ask her out. But as a freshman, working up the courage to ask out his first college date was not something that came easy. He finally got the nerve to call her and ask her out. Linda was cordial and cool in her reply as she said, "Well, I appreciate the offer, but on Saturday night, I need to write a paper." There were several ways Evan had to assess this statement. The most optimistic was that Linda was under stress and needed to get some work accomplished. However, this was his first collegiate experience in asking for a date, and he was in no mood to be optimistic. His immediate assessment was that she was saying a resounding "no," and his application of the answer was to lower his self-esteem by about twenty notches. Was he as unattractive as he felt? Would no one ever want to go out with him? Was he destined to be a bachelor for eternity? Of course not, but Evan's assessment of the response was colored by his lack of dating experience.

Evan later learned that three other guys on his dormitory floor also had asked Linda out in the last two weeks only to be rejected as well. Consequently, the coloring of his own assessment and application of her response changed with the new information. The point is that we *always* reduce information by filtering it through the situation we find ourselves in as well as through our past experiences.

Virtually every salesperson and consultant has experienced the temptation to make immediate application and assessment without recognizing the reduction that is occurring. A potential client, for example, reacts negatively to one of your proposals. The temptation is to make immediate application: "They have rejected my proposal." However, just because the client is responding in a certain way now, does not necessarily mean the proposal was not a good one—although this is always a possibility.

What it means for us is that we need to work at making sure in our assessment and application that we have not reduced from our thinking the facts concerning the client's current day. She may be under stress at the moment, too busy to give it the time required, frustrated or confused by the proposal, too tired to think properly, or any of a number of other possibilities. Coming back on another day might prompt a different reaction—maybe even a sale. The key to listening at this phase is learning to recognize that we do not always have all the information needed to make an assessment—even when we think we have. There is simply too much that we do not know.

The last phase in the listening process is the reaction to the speaker. Listening does not end with simply perceiving, assessing, and applying what has been said. Our reaction often determines whether the speaker feels as if we have been listening. This phase deals with *how* we react to the messages that we receive.

Brad, the executive director of a small nonprofit corporation, experienced a situation that demonstrates the importance of *how* we react to the messages we receive. Several employees came to him about their department head, Tony. They complained that Tony wasn't hearing them. Brad's impulse was to send Tony to a seminar for training in the perception stage of listening so that he could learn how to "listen" to the people in his department.

What Brad really needed was awareness and training not only in the "perception step," but also in the listening that occurs in the "reaction step." Tony thought he was listening to people when often he was hearing and remembering words. Tony was not demonstrating that he was listening to what people were saying. His mind said that he had heard and reacted appropriately, but his behavior demonstrated a reduction that was limiting his reaction. We instructed Brad as follows.

In the 1980s researchers found that what you do, both verbally and nonverbally, while listening affects the people who are speaking. For example, if you remain passive during a conversation and give no feedback, you may be perceived as not listening regardless of how well you actually are. So as we explained to Brad, when employees were speaking to Tony, his communication behavior said, "I am here, but I am not listening to you." As a result, until Tony was made to recognize that when he was reducing his reaction behavior until it was almost unreadable (nonexistent), he was being seen as not listening to what was being said.

The other side of the same coin was that if Tony did not match (actually mirror) what was being said with the verbal and nonverbal signals of the employees, he was likely to interact in a way that was less than adequate for the employees. In these situations the chances of Tony attaching a faulty meaning to the employees' messages would be much greater.

Consequently, what we told Brad was that he needed to focus on Tony's ability to "react" to the verbal and nonverbal communication behavior of employees with appropriate verbal and nonverbal actions. It was Tony's reaction behaviors that seemed to be critical to creating a productive, positive, rewarding listening atmosphere with employees. Brad reported to us that once Tony became more sensitive to his reaction behaviors, realized what he was doing, and changed his behavior appropriately, employees commented on the dramatic change in circumstances they experienced. They felt Tony had become much more responsive to their needs—sensitive and caring.

They clearly indicated in their remarks that reaction behaviors are critical to creating a solid listening atmosphere with employees.

Just knowing the three phases of listening helps us to understand the complexity of what occurs in any communication situation. It can help us because it breaks apart a process that we often respond to as a whole. With the process divided, it helps us look for problems, like Tony's, in any of the parts. Knowing where the problem lies, it is easier to suggest ways to correct it. It should be clear in these last four chapters that listening is not a singular process. There is much more to listening than simply hearing someone else's words.

The three phases of listening:

Perception ➤ **Assessment and Application** ➤ **Reaction**

Now it should be easy to see what some of the benefits of effective listening are. In the next section, we discuss how managers can listen to improve the work environment.

PART THREE

HOW CAN MANAGERS LISTEN TO IMPROVE THE WORK ENVIRONMENT?

CHAPTER 9

Why Is Listening Related To Your Business Survival?

"'Hell, Toto, this ain't Kansas,'" was a sign on Will Rogers' desk, according to an article in *Newsweek* (July 18, 1988). But this was not the Will Rogers we first think of when we hear the name. The article continued, "Will Rogers was the captain of what he called 'the most sophisticated ship in the world...' At the helm of the USS Vincennes, one of the Navy's 10 new Aegis cruisers, Rogers had entered the world of high-tech warfare. His command post, according to the article, "was below decks in a Combat Information Center dominated by four huge blue computer screens. He and his crew could see nothing but what the software showed them: a glowing line representing an Iranian aircraft coming ever closer. The state-of-the-art systems gave Rogers ambiguous information and just seven minutes to weigh it. The lives of 357 crew members, his own life, and the survival of his ship hung in the balance."

Often the world of the organization is compared with warfare. "We are on the attack," is one example. "Those employees are on the front lines," may be another. A third could be, "That plan got shot down." The metaphors of war often reflect the feelings of those trying to survive in a world where the quality and quantity of information one receives can mean the difference between life and death in the organizational environment.

The case of the USS Vincennes is an excellent example of how inadequate and ambiguous information coupled with combat stress means the difference between life and death. Organizations and businesses also face life-and-death decisions.

If you are not convinced that life and death decisions take place regularly in organizations, look at the 1986 and 1987 reports from Dun & Bradstreet on business failures. Their report directly reflects this fact. The first reason for business failures, according to the report, is a lack of capital. But, the second reason most businesses fail has nothing to do with externally controlled variables such as high interest rates, insufficient profits, unfair competition, or similar factors. Rather, the second reason has to do with internally controlled variables such as incompetence and lack of managerial experience. These are internal problems that potentially could have been solved with better information. And this information could have been received through better listening. Believe it?

In 1983, Bennett and Olney surveyed 100 "Fortune 500" companies. What they wanted to discover was the role of communication in the life of their business executives. The survey showed that listening was ranked as the second most serious problem frequently encountered. But do executives recognize the problem?

In a study done on the problems of small business and possible sources of assistance, Franklin and Goodwin (1983) surveyed a number of both large and small businesses. Their findings were revealing. When business owners listed *their* top five problems, all of them dealt with external variables, or things like governmental problems, that were beyond their control. Yet the data on organizational failures, according to Franklin and Goodwin, suggests that managers are focusing on the wrong problems. Instead of focusing on the external variables, they should be concerned with internal or controllable variables. We would suggest that listening effectiveness is one of these!

How important is listening? According to a study of Illinois manufacturing firms, 50 percent of the respondents ranked listening skills as a deficiency in employees. This same study concluded that the most deficient area of skills among employees in manufacturing firms is in the area of listening (Meister and Reisch 1978). In a 1974 study of practitioners in business and industry, listening was the largest time-consuming, on-the-job activity (Swanda and Weinrauch 1976).

In a survey of 1,000 personnel managers listed as members of "The American Society of Personnel Administrators," respondents indicated that interpersonal and human relations skills, including effective listening, are the most important factors or skills for successful job performance. In the same study, researchers found that personnel managers ranked "Ability to listen effectively" as the fourth most important factor or skill in an ideal management profile—meaning those characteristics these personnel managers think any high-quality manager should possess. The top three above listening were: working well with others one-on-one (which may depend on effective listening); ability to gather accurate information (which often is dependent on effective listening); and working well in small groups (where listening is of crucial importance). (Curtis, Winsor, and Stephens, 1989.)

It is clear that businesses need to focus their attention on internal variables such as gaining information and assistance rather than on blaming external variables. Knowledge is crucial for success! It stands to reason, then, that for organizations to gain the knowledge needed to sustain their lives, for managers to pass along and receive the information that makes up the lifeblood of organizations, good listening skills and abilities are crucial.

Effective listening is a problem in most companies. Organizations are in a constant battle to survive. It's easy to blame external problems and ignore the internal ones because the external problems are beyond control. The internal ones are so close that

1) they may not be recognized,
2) they may be traced to the very core (top) of the organizational chart, or
3) they may touch the nerves and sensitivities of too many people.

But by not treating the internal problems, it's like fighting a war by focusing completely on the other side's weapons without paying attention to your own. Regardless of their weapons, if yours don't work, then you are not going to survive.

We used the case of the USS Vincennes as an example of where inadequate and ambiguous information coupled with combat stress meant the difference between life and death. Most reading this remember the results. The USS Vincennes mistakenly shot down a passenger jet and many innocent lives were lost. The amount and kind of information received in the Combat Information Center, despite the sophistication of the equipment, was ambiguous. The point is that despite our best efforts, despite the quality of our information sources, errors can still occur. There are no guarantees. In retrospect, one could say that if the incoming plane had been a fighter jet, the USS Vincennes could have been lost entirely; so Will Rogers and his crew did their best with the information they had and saved themselves and the ship.

There is no doubt that listening is a valuable weapon and tool in business. Since you want to use every tool possible to gain valuable information—like the dependency of Will Rogers on his four huge blue computer screens—listening is important. Listening aids in the acquisition of knowledge and in the management of people. But what often happens is, at the moment you need information, you talk instead of listen. Remember, knowledge is crucial to success: Listen to Win!

CHAPTER 10

Why Is Listening Related To Your Survival?

"Nonsense, they couldn't hit an elephant at this dist——." These were the last words of Union General John Sedgwick, as he chose not to listen to his field officer's warnings and instead raised his head above a parapet during the Civil War's Battle of the Wilderness.

There are times in life when we want to hope that certain things are true. We want to believe that good will win over evil, that people who work hard get rewarded for their efforts, that there is a payoff for the work that they do. We would like to believe that good quality actually makes a difference in both product and performance. But often we simply do not have the evidence that demonstrates the truth of these hopes.

There recently was a study reported in a scholarly journal. It should have received attention, but it didn't. It wasn't flashy enough to be highlighted on "Good Morning America." It didn't rate a spot in *USA Today.* But it should have! Why? Because it is one of those things that you want to hope is true, but have never seen any hard evidence of its truth.

The study, "Listening, Communication Abilities, and Success at Work," by Beverly Davenport Sypher, Robert Bostrom, and Joy Hart Seibert, researches the role that listening plays in the success of employees. The last paragraph should echo in every workplace in America: "What we can conclude from this study is that listening is related to other communication abilities and to success at work. Better listeners held higher-level positions and were promoted more often than those with less developed listening abilities."

We would like to believe that people who are perceived as being good listeners will get somewhere in life. That they will not only survive on the job but be respected and promoted for their ability to listen and assimilate information. We would like to believe that people who listen will be tangibly recognized for having this ability. We would like to see that just once the little guy wins the fight, the underdog wins the big game, the nerd makes a million, and the guy who listens actually gets promoted.

Cynics would say that this is just one study and that we need more proof. Academics can argue over the fine points of the methods used to reach the conclusions in the report. Even the authors of the article acknowledge that replication of the study would give them more confidence. It does not necessarily prove anything. It may be a fluke. BUT, it may not be!

According to the same study, of 25 different studies focusing on critical employment skills, the one skill mentioned most often was listening. Another study with training and development managers in "Fortune 500" companies demonstrated that managers believed poor listening was one of the most important problems facing them (Hunt and Cusella 1983). Not only that, they believed that ineffective listening led to poor performance or low productivity.

It may just be that listening is related to your success. It may be that General Sedgwick would have lived to fight another day had he listened to his field officers. In fact, this just may be the tip of the iceberg. Where information often is the key to life or death for organizations, listening may be the key to obtaining and understanding information for individuals. People who listen just may have an edge over people who do not.

We have a colleague who was on temporary status with our organization this past year. She wanted a permanent position in the coming year. She is always talking with someone. She is nonstop in her discussions on a variety of issues with every individual who seems to cross her path. She is always immersed in conversation. But when you talk with her, she seems to be thinking about what she was just discussing or some great new idea.

Forget about engaging in serious conversation concerning something that is affecting your productivity or her productivity. Although, she is always nodding her head, smiling, and saying "uh huh, uh huh, I see what you mean," her next words are, "You know I've been thinking about…" and it's off down a new road that she wants to travel. Was she listening? Only enough to figure out how she could take control of the conversation. Is she productive? No. Did she get a permanent job with the organization this coming year? No.

Maybe her listening abilities are directly related to her productivity, and maybe they aren't. But when a study like this one comes out, when an individual like this doesn't get promoted, you begin to realize that maybe there *is* a relationship between listening and personal success. Everybody wants an edge in the job market. Everybody wants to succeed. Everybody wants to know what it takes to be successful. No one wants to be shot down. Listening is one edge that you can learn! Effective listening *does* make an important difference.

Fortunately, most ineffective, weak, or nonexistent listening does not result in sudden death as in the case of General Sedgwick. If it did, and if it occurred on a consistent basis, listening effectiveness would be a topic that would have a section all its own in today's bookstores. Who knows when the time is exactly right for effective listening? Since we cannot know, we should practice effective listening skills all the time. If we do, these skills will become habitual and practiced all the time. Then, life-and-death situations become life situations only. At that point all that need concern us is the *quality* of life. Most people are interested in adding to the quality of their lives.

To add to the quality of your life, then, start now. Listen to Win!

CHAPTER 11

Why Do You Need Ways To Create A Positive Listening Environment?

The biggest obstacle to creating a positive listening environment is easy to see, but hard to change. The problem is most people think they already are good listeners. Yet, often they don't keep quiet long enough to find out if they are or not. How many times have you heard someone say, "I really am not a very good listener," or "I'm a great talker, but a poor listener." It is common to hear people admit they don't feel comfortable talking in front of others, that they are shy, or that they are not assertive enough. But rarely do you hear people admit they don't feel comfortable listening to people. To admit they aren't good listeners is to imply they are focused on themselves and don't care about others.

Imagine working with someone like John. John is a great talker, but a lousy listener. He interrupts you mid-sentence to complete your thought and then make his point. He rarely asks you a question about what you are saying. He always has something to say after you speak because while you were speaking he was deciding what he was going to say. He may or may not remember what you have discussed. And, even if he remembers, that does not mean he understands your perspective. He would describe himself as friendly and articulate.

We all know someone like John. And we are frustrated by his or her lack of listening skills. Chances are, John has had problems at work. In fact, he is probably frustrating for his boss. Why don't John's coworkers, or why doesn't his boss, tell him to listen for a change?

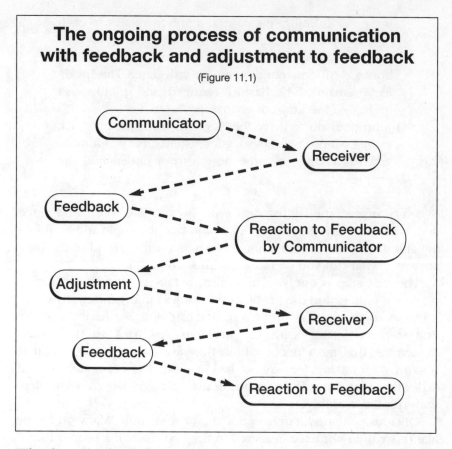

The ongoing process of communication with feedback and adjustment to feedback

(Figure 11.1)

Communicator

Receiver

Feedback

Reaction to Feedback by Communicator

Adjustment

Receiver

Feedback

Reaction to Feedback

Why doesn't John make any effort to change? There are four reasons, and these reasons illustrate the circular process that creates problems. *(See Figure 11.1.)*

(1) John is rewarded for talking rather than for listening.
(2) Besides wanting to tell him to listen every now and then, John's boss and fellow employees do not understand the listening process well enough to give him feedback.
(3) John's boss either ignores the problem, or when the boss must confront it, she calls the problem by a different name—being out of touch with employees and customers, not being able to get along with people, poor planning, poor decision-making, being aloof and distant, the list is endless. This is not to say that each of these different problems is simply another way of say-

ing poor listening. Poor listening often relates to each
of these problems; in fact, it may be the root or core
problem that creates the others. John's coworkers and
boss are still frustrated several months later. The "problem" remains. John has not changed, and it looks as if
he has no intention of changing.

(4) John does not receive feedback on his listening skills,
so he assumes that he is a good listener. He is not motivated to change because he does not understand the
problem.

Every organization must deal with people like John. And since
duct taping mouths isn't acceptable (and people would still be thinking about what they were going to say when they got rid of the tape
anyway), what can you do to deal with such people?

The first step is one you have already taken: awareness. That is,
when we understand the problem that occurs in organizations when
it comes to the circular process of non-listening, we have taken the
first step in dealing with the problem. Go back to the circle.
Remember that most people think they are good listeners. John is
rewarded for talking. He assumes he is a good listener because no one
says otherwise. John is not motivated to change. How do you deal
with this basic problem?

Obviously the problem has gone on for some time. Many problems
like this would not have occurred in the first place if a proper listening atmosphere had been created. Businesses where managers have
worked to create and maintain listening climates are less likely to
experience problems like the one with John. The real question, or at
least the first question, should be how to create that initial, preliminary atmosphere. This will be discussed further in the next chapter;
but for now, let's make a number of brief comments here to help you
create a listening atmosphere:

- Everyone on your staff should be aware of your genuine
  interest in them as individuals.
- Know both names of all the people in your department,
  in your division, on your staff, or in your group.
- Develop the proper amount of friendliness without over-
  familiarity.
- Go out of the way to be helpful to others on things that
  don't necessarily relate to the job.
- Be prepared to go all out for your people if the facts war-

rant it, even if it may mean some inconvenience for you.
- Go out of the way, as much as appropriate, to establish mutual interests with subordinates.
- Keep the communication lines sufficiently open and used, so that the times you seek out contacts with subordinates are not something special and ominous.
- In the interviews and other interpersonal contacts you have with others, subordinates included, create a relaxed, unhurried air that helps others feel at ease and emphasizes your receptivity.

If you are truly concerned about others—and this will show through the above methods—you are modeling the kind of climate you would like others to establish. That is how people problems like that of John get solved early. John will begin—early in his work with the company—to see how others operate. Also, when he doesn't fit in, it will be easier to gently nudge and suggest because the atmosphere is already in place.

But there is a second problem revealed above that is less easy to solve. How do you effectively deal with John's problem, after the fact, and avoid alienating or antagonizing him? John is a good worker, and you don't want to lose him. The problem clearly exists already, but it is serious enough to be dealt with, too. Let us offer some suggestions:
- Be sensitive to his communication problems.
- Strive to be a good listener for him.
- Make him feel comfortable in communicating with you.
- Reveal encouragement, support, openness, and honesty.
- Be sympathetic, compassionate, and gentle.
- Show preferences for John's similarities and emphasize things John likes.
- Convey approval and invite communication.
- Reveal relaxed composure. Come across as poised, relaxed, calm, cool, and controlled.
- Reveal immediacy through verbal closeness by using messages that encourage communication like "I see what you mean...," "Tell me more...," "That is a good point...," or "I think so too..."
- Understand, support, and use the principle of reciprocity. That is, show a tendency to imitate the behavior of John while with him. This will open him up, get him to trust you, and reveal strong empathy.

With the proper atmosphere created one-on-one with John, it will be easier to talk honestly and directly with him. It will not be possible to facilitate the kind of change in John without first attempting to set up the proper atmosphere. It is better to have the atmosphere in place first rather than having to create it after a problem occurs, but John needs gentle persuasion, not commands; he needs kind, cooperative assistance rather than dogmatic, judgmental advice. Be patient, be sincere, take time, and show care and concern, and it is possible that John will come around.

CHAPTER 12

How Can You Combat Poor Listening Behavior?

What is unique about this chapter is its specific, practical nature. In the last chapter we gave a wide variety of brief suggestions for establishing a listening atmosphere both as part of a company climate and in dealing with specific individuals. Here we not only talk about specific problems, but we offer specific solutions as well. Also, we discuss rewards for good behavior. Although we are talking about how managers can combat poor listening behavior, remember that the information applies to you, as a listening manager, as well.

There are four primary ways to create a listening environment. First, we must identify poor listening behaviors. Second, we must give listening feedback. Third, we must confront listening problems and finally, we need to use nonverbal communication to reinforce our points. In this chapter we will discuss each of these elements.

BE ABLE TO IDENTIFY POOR LISTENING BEHAVIORS

The first step is knowledge. It will be far easier to identify poor listening behaviors if you understand the listening process. In Figure 12.1 there is a list of common problems that occur with people who are poor listeners. Study this list to see how many of these characteristics fit you and your listening style. Notice how common the problems are?

What are the common problems that occur with people who are poor listeners?

(FIGURE 12.1)

- Prejudging
- Close-minded
- Distorting messages
- Laziness
- Opinionated
- Oversimplifying
- Filtering out undesirable messages
- Phasing in and out
- Not listening to whole message
- Letting our biases determine what we hear
- Prejudicial listening
- Not trying to see another's point of view
- Not eliminating physical barriers
- Interrupting speaker
- Inattentive
- Boredom
- Not trying to understand thoughts *and* feelings
- Pretending to listen
- Insincerity

- Not combating sources of noise
- Listening only to bits and pieces of information
- Daydreaming
- Not recognizing that we think faster than we speak
- Only listening when it requires little effort
- Not assuming some value in another's message
- Avoiding difficult messages
- Not exerting enough energy to listen well
- Not providing feedback
- Judging delivery as content
- Sharpening or increasing importance of messages
- Tuning out because of distractions
- Not eliminating psychological barriers

Take this list and circulate it among the people who work in your organization. Do it in a humorous manner; do it in a straightforward fashion—whatever works best for you. But do it! Make people aware of specific listening behaviors. This is important.

The first step in creating a listening environment is being able to identify behaviors that indicate when listening is a problem or when good listening is taking place. Also, there is a good chance that by simply calling people's attention to specific behaviors, the awareness will help listening behaviors improve—not to mention potentially helping your own listening improve. Remember, people will be looking carefully at you. What we said about modeling a good, positive, support-ive listening climate in the last chapter applies here.

GIVE LISTENING FEEDBACK

The second step is to learn to give listening feedback. Again, we find the duct tape temptation strong with certain individuals. But putting duct tape over someone's mouth generally creates a defensive reac-tion! *(See Figure 12.2.)* This list of phrases will help you respond in a way that is not defensive. Hopefully it provides a starting point for your own development of appropriate responses. Remember, people cannot change what they do not know. By giving specific feedback, you are helping them improve their listening behaviors and you are encouraging them to listen to your ideas.

CONFRONT LISTENING PROBLEMS

Don Warwick, a noted organizational development writer, has this to say, "You get what you reward, and you deserve what you tolerate." People gravitate to what they enjoy and to things that give them rewards. This is one time where if you ignore listening problems, they will not go away. Silence is like a reward, and if listening prob-lems are tolerated, they may get worse.

This is very familiar in classrooms. When negative student behav-ior occurs and nothing is said about it, it is as if the negative behav-ior is sanctioned. Then when another student does the exact same thing and gets punished or reprimanded for it, what is the first thing the student says? "Tommy did it, and you didn't say anything!" And the second student is correct!

Communication patterns are not easily changed, and by not acknowledging the problem or by calling it a different name, there is no possibility for change. Listening problems cannot be ignored. If they are, then you deserve what you tolerate.

Find ways to reward good listening. In Figure 12.3 there is a list of interpersonal rewards that you can use to encourage people to listen to you. Remember Warwick's statement, "You get what you reward, but you deserve what you tolerate."

Non-defensive feedback phrases
(Figure 12.2)

"How do you feel about the situation?"

"Maybe we should look at this idea together with no predetermined attitudes or solutions."

"Let's be open, straightforward, and honest about this situation. The best way to deal with situations like this is by being direct."

"I think I know how you feel. Maybe we could talk about the problem a bit more. Sharing feelings like this may help."

"Isn't it terrific that we can discuss problems from the same viewpoint? To push aside our differences like this allows us to have a meeting of minds."

"There are no certain ways to approach this situation. Let's just try something, and if it doesn't work, we'll try something else."

USE NONVERBAL COMMUNICATION TO REINFORCE THE POINT

You are sitting in a meeting and Sam interrupts the speaker. Everyone turns to look at Sam while he speaks. Nonverbally, they have just given him the floor and rewarded him for the interruption. Now imagine this: Sam interrupts and as the senior manager you do not look at Sam but continue to look at the previous speaker with interest. Sam realizes that you are not focused on what he is saying, and soon he will relinquish the floor. Nonverbally you have communicated to Sam that you are not listening to him and that he interrupted an important thought. You make the point without saying a word.

Nonverbal communication gives feedback about listening. As was listed in Figure 12.1, nonverbal responses are often indicators of poor listening behaviors. During conversations we rely on nonverbal responses more than on verbal responses to tell us if people are listening to us.

Think of nonverbal communication as a weapon to make a point.

Learn to use nonverbal communication as a means of encouraging listening. Your nonverbal behavior, particularly in a meeting like the example with Sam, reinforces that you want people to listen, even when you are not the boss. Look at Figure 12.3. These are a few ways that you can make the point without verbally jabbing at someone.

If you combine nonverbal feedback with verbal responses, you can strongly reinforce the point. Back at the meeting, let's say that you are not the boss. When Sam interrupts, you can still hold your gaze on the speaker for a few moments longer. Chances are that Sam began speaking, like most of us, by scanning the room for eye contact as he started. Your initial nonverbal cue told him you were still thinking about what was being said before he interrupted. As he gives you eye contact while he speaks, look at Sam, but then immediately look back to the other speaker. You are connecting, visually, Sam with the other speaker. Now, looking back at Sam, get eye contact, lean forward slightly, and open your mouth as if you are ready to speak. You could even begin a gesture if it is comfortable. You are giving Sam the signal that you are about to speak.

When Sam is finished, call everyone's attention back to the previous speaker by looking at her. Mention that when you were listening to her speak, you were not sure she had finished her thought, and you wanted to be certain you understood her point. This verbally and nonverbally signals four things:

(1) she was interrupted,
(2) you were listening to her,
(3) what she had to say was of value, and
(4) interruptions are not rewarded.

As you combine verbal responses with nonverbal reactions, you are sending a message that listening is important and will be rewarded. Remember that in a group while people are speaking, you must acknowledge the fact that you are listening to them. If you do not, you risk communicating to others that what they have to say is not important. When people talk more than they listen, communicating nonverbally that they are talking too much is a critical tool.

Interpersonal Rewards to Encourage Listening
(Figure 12.3)

Most feedback comes in the form of nonverbal messages. Do not overlook the effectiveness of a puzzled face, a wide smile, or a clear head nod.

- Phrases designed to affirm understanding:

  "That does make sense ... "
  "I see what you're saying ... "
  "That seems like a reasonable position ... "

- Phrases designed to gain further elaboration:

  "Perhaps these ideas require a little more thought ... "
  "I see what you're saying, but I need a little more information on this ... "
  "Could you expand on that idea?"

- Phrases designed to gain clarity before giving further feedback:

  "Let me see if I have this correct ... "
  "Is this what you're saying? ... "
  "If I have heard you right, you're saying ... "
  "Correct me if I'm wrong here ... "

- Phrases designed to be sensitive, supportive, open-minded, helpful, and specific:

  "I understand your intent here, but what I don't understand is ... "
  "I see where you're coming from. What may be missing is ... "
  "OK, if what you're saying is right, then ... "

- Phrases designed to reveal a nonhostile intent and yet still disagree:

  "In all due respect ... "
  "I can see how you reached that conclusion, but ... "
  "I'm not trying to be deliberately difficult, but ... "
  "I was on the verge of a similar conclusion myself, until ... "
  "While your observation makes sense to me, the facts seem to indicate ... "
  "I wish I could agree with you, however ... "

SUMMARY

Creating a listening atmosphere begins with people! Remember, most people think they are good listeners, but most people don't listen to others long enough to find out. If you want to create a listening atmosphere, start with knowledge, and move to feedback about behavior. People do not like change. Rarely will they change without reward. We have offered a variety of potential rewards that not only tell people we are listening, but let's them know that we care. Remember the quote from Don Warwick, "We get what we reward and deserve what we tolerate." If you want to create a positive listening atmosphere, be a good listener!

PART FOUR

HOW CAN MANAGERS LISTEN SO EMPLOYEES WILL SPEAK?

CHAPTER 13

How Do You Create Listening Problems?

John R. Houghton, 52, is chief executive of Corning Glass Works. John is a model of how to develop and communicate a leader's vision. According to an article in *Fortune* (October 24, 1988), Houghton's campaign for quality at Corning Glass helped create a cultural change. Prior to Houghton, there were scattered suggestion boxes around his plants. Employees who put forward something useful would receive small checks months later. This system led to considerable backbiting and jealousy because employees bickered over whose ideas best merited reward. Even worse, the system of suggestion boxes failed to produce a steady stream of good ideas.

So Houghton found a better way. Managers repeatedly encouraged employees to make suggestions. Good ideas were adopted more quickly; but not only that, the person who made the suggestion was often asked for assistance in—and became involved in the process of—implementing his or her suggestions. The result was far more employees piping up. They found their satisfaction alone is sufficient reward. In the article, Houghton said, "There is a much more open atmosphere. We get five times as many suggestions, we act on 40 times as many of them—and we don't give money."

One reason why John R. Houghton is a respected manager of people is because he came up with a way to listen to his employees that was both effective and efficient. It is one thing to communicate the vision and quite another to demonstrate that your ideas are not the only ones that will make up the vision.

Contrast the example of Houghton to that of Tom Miller, a candidate for the position of department chair. We sat in a committee meeting where Tom was being interviewed for this position. The meeting started with the committee chair asking Tom to tell the committee a little about his past. For the next fifty minutes Tom talked without stopping. In the next two interviews with Tom, the committee members quickly learned that if they wanted to get in a question, they would have to interrupt him. At the end of the day, one of our colleagues turned to us and said, "His examples of how he helped several of his people succeed were good. But it makes you wonder if they succeeded because he was doing all the talking, and they just followed orders, or if Tom actually took the time to listen to their ideas and then help them succeed. I'm not sure I want a chair who only talks about his own ideas."

Tom was suspect. Why? Because he failed to demonstrate that he knew how to listen. Every leader soon realizes that providing vision and meaning for an organization requires communication. And to be effective, communication requires listening. Communication is not a one-way, unilateral process.

So why don't employees just naturally tell you what's on their mind? What's the problem? Why do we have a chapter on listening so that employees will speak? There are three reasons:

1) Most of us don't know when to shut our mouths so others can speak. Tom is a good example. Put in a position of authority or visibility or responsibility, most people talk too much. Often, when we do shut our mouth, the way we listen is part of the problem.

2) Most employees do not have the encouragement from management to speak. Look what happened with the suggestion boxes. Often, employees feel inferior, intimidated, put down, or frightened. Encouragement is more than lip service; it is providing multiple channels for employees to speak.

3) Often, employees do not trust management's response when they do speak—perhaps for good reason. That is why establishing the proper listening environment first is so important. It builds trust. Effective listening emerges naturally from its own breeding ground, just as a seed emerges from the soil with the proper amount of sun, moisture, and nutrition.

THE WAY MANAGEMENT LISTENS MAY BE THE PROBLEM

One reason that employees do not speak up is found in the way management listens. Often, managers use a style of listening called "recall listening." "Recall listening" focuses on remembering what was said. This form of listening hears what was said, is extremely objective in understanding what was said, yet does not give feedback that communicates to others that they have been listened to. It seldom goes beyond the senses (hearing) to what others feel (the emotions) or think (the intellectual). As we discussed in Chapter 5, listening is not hearing.

Often, management will listen to a new idea, but in the evaluation process decide not to use it. Matt, an organizational specialist, was working with Lowell, an employer, who had listening problems. Matt was put in a situation where Lowell and another key employee, Randall, met to discuss their differences. Randall complained that Lowell did not hear him in the meeting the previous week. Lowell, on the other hand, could tell Randall exactly what he had said, and proceeded to do so. But Randall still felt that Lowell really had not been listening, since he did not see any results or reactions from Lowell.

Randall felt as though he had not really been heard. It was Matt who pointed out to Lowell that he had employed "recall listening." Matt also said that Randall's response to recall listening is typical. It makes you feel as if you haven't really been heard because feedback is lacking. There is no responsiveness. It is as if Lowell did not really care about Randall's contributions.

How do you check to see if you are using recall listening? Answer the following two questions: First, do you focus on only remembering what was said? Second, do you give feedback that communicates to the speaker that he or she has been listened to? This includes verbal feedback such as summarizing what you have heard and nonverbal feedback such as nods of the head.

The answer to the first question, "Do you focus on remembering what was said?" of course, should be "No." The answer to the second question, "Do you give feedback that communicates to the speaker that he or she has been listened to?" of course, should be "Yes," if you want to avoid recall listening. Recall listening is a negative form of listening when practiced by itself. It fails to reveal the listener's true feelings. It fails to indicate caring and concern. If removes the human element from the listening situation.

CHAPTER 14

How Can You Use Active Listening For Listening Effectiveness?

As we saw in the preceding chapter, "recall listening" is likely to create listening problems. Some people might say "recall listening" is better than no listening at all—and we are sure they are right. We would all prefer some listening to no listening. But there is a better kind of listening with more positive results—every time! It is the kind of listening that offers communicators a response. "Active listening" focuses on giving feedback to speakers, paraphrasing what is said, and giving nonverbal responses.

We were at a business party and one of us was talking to the partner of a company. When we walked away from the conversation, we were amazed at what had happened. While talking to this partner, we realized something important. We were the entire focus of her conversation. When she talked to us, there were no other distractions. She made us feel special, privileged, one-of-a-kind. It was as if she turned a spotlight on us, and we basked in the warm glow of the spotlight. It was such a unique experience. It was clear to both of us why she had reached the position in the company that she had. She was a powerful and effective listener—an active listener. She knew the importance of the response.

Active listening is the kind of listening that lets speakers know they have been listened to. In two organizational studies (Hunt and Cusella 1983; Rhodes 1985), people consistently rated "active listening" skills higher than "recall listening" skills. People want verbal and nonverbal reinforcement that emphasizes not only the hearing and remembering, but, most of all, they want a response! The key in active listening is the response.

Active listening skills demand interaction. Think of it this way. You go to McDonald's because you are hungry; you want food. You don't just want the people behind the counter to simply remember what you ordered, you want them to act on what they heard. And the sooner the better!

In a period of time in which the need for immediate gratification is high, our listening skills must reflect this reality. Employees want to receive instant feedback about what they said or what they suggested rather than just knowing that it will be remembered or "taken into account." That is precisely why instant prepared foods are a billion-dollar-a-year business. That is why the "instant lottery" works! We can have our food or our money almost instantly.

Obviously, combining recall listening and active listening is critical for long- and short-term success. In this way, it isn't one or the other, but both working together. Effective managers make use of both. It's like the old saying, "There is a time and place for everything." But, today, the immediate response is critical to both speaker and listener. Employees who receive instant feedback will likely perceive management to be listening based on their behaviors (active listening) rather than on passive memorization (recall listening).

Just as there are different types of food in restaurants, there are different types of feedback as well. For example, restaurant meals often begin with an appetizer. So, too, can feedback begin with a small, fairly simple response like eye contact. When providing feedback, a respondent does not have to immediately give the speaker the whole answer to issues that are being raised by the speaker. In fact, it would be an insult at times if you did. For example, when a speaker begins talking, in most cases you need to listen for a short time just to get the complete message. To provide a full answer like, "Yes, I agree," may be premature, irresponsible, inappropriate, or impossible! Sometimes things need time and attention. More important is for respondents to react or act in a fashion that acknowledges individuals and their statements and lets them know they are being listened to. Remember, it's the response!

When we are listening to others, we need to check to make sure we are listening actively. We can do this by asking ourselves three questions:

1) Are you giving feedback to speakers as they speak?
2) Are you paraphrasing what the other person is saying? (Saying again what others have said—in different words, let's them know their ideas are being received and received accurately.)
3) Are you using ongoing nonverbal communication to provide responses to the messages being sent?

The important element is giving others a response to what they have said. This is not necessarily a verbal answer to whatever their request, concern, idea, or suggestion may be. Rather, it is a reaction that demonstrates they have been listened to. This response is the essence—the core—of active listening.

CHAPTER 15

How Can The H.E.A.R. Method Help You Listen Better?

Vince: "I will meet you at the City Center at 4:30 P.M. sharp."

Trish: "You'll be at the main entrance of the City Center this afternoon at 4:30 P.M."

Vince: "Yes, I will meet you just inside the main entrance in case of rain. You can still make it, can't you?"

Trish: "Yes, I can make it. Everything has worked out, and I will be there. Meeting inside is a good idea; I heard it was supposed to rain. Is the agenda the same?"

Vince: "Yes, the agenda is the same. I'm glad we'll have a chance to talk about this issue."

Trish: "I look forward to talking with you."

We will refer back to this dialogue between Vince and Trish momentarily. It provides a good example of the use of the H.E.A.R. method of listening which we explain in this chapter. First, notice the difference between "recall" and "active" listening outlined in Figure 15.1. More importantly, notice the individual items that you can use to give effective feedback without suddenly taking over the talking—something most people with power are tempted to do! *(See Figure 15.2.)*

This brief review of recall and active listening, which were discussed in the last two chapters, serves as a useful introduction to the H.E.A.R. method. The H.E.A.R. method of "active" listening is simply a useful tool. We have used the acronym H.E.A.R. as a prompt—a way

Recall listening	**Active listening**
➡ Focuses on remembering what was said by the speaker	➡ Focuses on giving feedback to the speaker
➡ Hears what was said	➡ Listens to speaker
➡ Physical response without emotions and intellect	➡ Emotional and intellectual response
➡ Objective approach	➡ Subjective approach
➡ Provides no response	➡ Is response oriented
➡ A negative form of listening	➡ A positive form of listening
➡ Involves no paraphrasing	➡ Involves paraphrasing
➡ Gives no nonverbal cues	➡ Provides nonverbal cues

(Figure 15.1)

to remind yourself to use it when needed. *H*ear the message. *E*ngage in summarizing what you heard the individual saying. *A*sk questions about what you heard (don't forget to let them give answers to your questions). *R*eact appropriately. Either tell them what you think of what they said, or tell them when you will get back to them about what you think of what they said.

The four steps comprising the the H.E.A.R. method provide feedback, clarification, and encouragement to the speaker. Using them effectively gives individuals a feeling that what they said was listened to and worthy of a response. Once again, it offers strong evidence that the responding person is sincere, cares, shows concern, and can be trusted.

Notice our opening dialogue between Vince and Trish. This conversation represents effective use of the H.E.A.R. method. As Vince sets up the meeting, it is clear that Trish has heard what is said. Trish first engages in summarizing, and she adds the element about meeting at the main entrance. Next, Trish summarizes what Vince has said, and then she engages in questioning at the same time she asks him if the agenda is the same. Finally, she reacts when she says, "I look forward to talking to you." Notice, too, that Vince follows very closely the H.E.A.R. method. That is what makes this dialogue so effective. It is unlikely either has missed any part of the conversation and that the meeting will take place exactly as planned.

One last comment about the types of nonverbal feedback management may use while listening. Studies have demonstrated that eye contact is the beginning of an interpersonal encounter. Facial and eye communication provide the "traffic signals" that help maintain a smooth flow of conversation. Communication through the eyes and face gives us insight into the emotions being expressed by the other person. One person has even said that the eyes are the gateway to the soul, which indicates how much importance this person gave to the eyes.

The point is this: People in power have a tendency to make eye contact more while speaking than while listening. The boss wants to make sure employees are listening, so he or she watches them while

---

Items you can use to give effective feedback without suddenly taking over the talking:

✓ Empathizing

✓ Building rapport

✓ Responding purposefully

✓ Redefining messages

✓ Responding nonverbally

✓ Taking physical notes

✓ Taking mental notes

✓ Sorting main ideas from details

✓ Avoiding prejudice and bias

✓ Reading nonverbal cues

✓ Identifying speaker's purpose

✓ Recalling information

✓ Distinguishing fact from fiction

✓ Creating a climate

✓ Distinguishing connotative from denotative meanings

✓ Asking questions

✓ Making appropriate references

✓ Paraphrasing

✓ Giving instructions

✓ Taking instructions

✓ Developing objectivity

✓ Getting the "real" message

✓ Learning to summarize orally

✓ Giving criticism

✓ Taking criticism

✓ Reading feedback

✓ Improving concentration

✓ Developing concentration

✓ Developing comprehension

✓ Separating ideas from personalities

✓ Synthesizing and summarizing

✓ Following directions

✓ Being open-minded and objective

✓ Giving non-evaluative feedback

(Figure 15.2)

---

speaking. On the other hand, people with low power have a tendency to make eye contact more while listening. Employees want to make sure they understand exactly what the boss said. It's a natural phenomena, right? *Wrong.*

It doesn't matter if you are the boss or not, the point is if you want employees to speak, send them cues that say, "I want to be sure I understand exactly what you are saying." This means making eye contact and looking at them just as much when *they* are speaking as when *you* are. This sends them a message about their importance and helps you improve your understanding of what is being said. Amazingly enough, if you are the boss, it is not as easy as it sounds!

But we need to begin by H.E.A.R.-*ing* the message. Do you H.E.A.R. the message?

- *H*ear the message.
- *E*ngage in summarizing.
- *A*sk questions.
- *R*eact appropriately.

To implement the H.E.A.R. method means you need to listen.

CHAPTER 16

How Can You Use A Positive Past To Forecast A Positive Future?

Leaders and managers do not operate in a vacuum. Trust and respect is built from past behaviors. That is why building the listening atmosphere as discussed in Chapters 11 and 12 is so important. Employees place a leader's current efforts at communication into the context of past encounters. It cannot be helped; it cannot be avoided. Current behavior establishes the criteria by which future behaviors will be judged (Lewis and Reinsch 1988). Past determines future!

An example of this is the physician who has seen many common ailments. As a result, when the patient comes in with what looks like a common problem, the doctor may interrupt the patient and finish his or her sentences with a description of the problem just to save time. The doctor may interrupt with the right answer several times without realizing it. Eventually the patient will come to think that the doctor knows everything, and he or she does not need to tell the doctor anything because he knows it already.

Later, when the patient is seriously ill, the doctor may be frustrated with diagnostic problems because of poor communication with this same patient. Unknowingly through poor listening behaviors, the doctor created the communication problem through the negative past behaviors he demonstrated.

When this happens in business and employers do not listen completely to employee problems, much time, energy, and money can be wasted. They may end up solving problems that do not exist, attacking only part of a much larger problem, or assuming certain problems have already been solved when they have not. Why? Because past experience tells the employee that the employer either already understood the problem or that the employer did not want to be bothered with a problem as minor as this one.

That is what positions of power, authority, and control can do. If the people in these positions do not develop a positive past by clearly demonstrating effective communication skills, then through their power, authority, and control, they are likely to intimidate subordinates. This can unwittingly drive away employees. It isn't the actual power, authority, and control—although it could be—it is the employees' perception of that power, authority, and control. It isn't what exists, but what they *think* exists that may cause problems. That is why people in these positions must continually try to compensate for the power, authority, and control they have—especially when effective listening is the goal.

The building-block effect that comes from past listening experiences forms the structure that builds communication relationships. For those who do not have a good listening track record, how people communicate with you in the present and future is going to be affected. Just as past habits can be negative, controlling, and restrictive, they can be positive as well. Fortunately poor habits can be changed, and good habits can be reinforced. As we discussed in Chapter 3, to change bad habits requires awareness, practice of new behaviors, and effort. If our past holds positive habits, we need to hone and polish those habits to reinforce them. We need to become aware of our behaviors.

Change-management specialists tell us that behaviors only become habits after we have practiced them for a minimum of thirty days. Now is the time to implement what you have just read and turn negative behaviors into positive habits. In Chapter 4, we discussed how you can begin changing habits.

The first step is by becoming aware of the building blocks. The second step is building a program for personal change. Because the process is so important we want to go over once again, this five-step model that aids in changing behavior:

1. Awareness of the problem or motive.
2. Motivation or desire to change.
3. A plan or way to achieve the goal.
4. Energy and commitment to put the plan into action.
5. A mental image or picture of you having completed the goal.

The point is that because most people do not listen well, they need to start establishing a positive past. It is likely they need to make some significant changes in their behaviors. But, as we previously noted, without some kind of a plan for change like the five-step model, it is likely that nothing at all will happen—except continuation of the same negative behaviors that have created the problems.

To understand your positive past, answer the following questions:

- Are you aware of your listening behaviors?
- Do you monitor what you do in listening situations?
- Do you want to change negative listening behaviors?

Remember: establishing a positive past begins when you listen.

CHAPTER 17

How Can You Avoid The Barriers To Effective Listening?

There are a number of barriers that may block an employee's willingness to speak in addition to management's listening style. In this chapter, we will concentrate on four of them:

1) Killing the messenger.
2) "This better be important."
3) The great way to kill loyalty.
4) "Who do I talk to?"

KILLING THE MESSENGER

One of the vivid images in the war with Iraq was General Schwarzkopf answering a question on why there was so little resistance by the Iraqi Army. His response was that soldiers who are afraid of being shot by their own officers simply do not fight well. In today's business world, one of the real fears of employees is "what will happen to me if I speak out." A number of profiles of people who spoke out have been featured on such television shows as "60 Minutes," "20/20," and "Prime Time."

The point is, in our society we don't like people who blow the whistle on problems. When we were kids we called them "tattletales," after a shorebird of the same name that makes frequent loud calls. In prisons they are known as "snitches." In the government they are known as informers. Even the names sound negative. Whatever they are called, we don't like to know about our mistakes and shortcomings, whether they are personal mistakes or company problems. Most of all, we don't like people whom we cannot trust—who are disloyal in any way. Often, when the information is in any way negative—or simply something we don't want to hear—it is easier to kill the messenger than to deal with the information.

Back to Iraq. Saddam Hussein chose to literally kill the messenger. When his generals disagreed with him or when people brought him news he didn't want to hear, he had them shot. As a result, he was unable to make effective decisions.

In company life, we have special ways of killing our messengers. When employees come to us repeatedly about problems, we may label them as having "a bad attitude." Another label we use is that they are "not being a team player." This occurs when employees have questions about a particular plan, process, or product and are hesitant to proceed until some questions are answered. As a result, employees get the message loud and clear. It is better not to speak, because management really doesn't want to listen.

While killing the messenger is tempting, it seldom enhances the information we receive. We need to remember that a businessperson's judgment is only as good as his or her information. When we kill the messengers, what information will we receive? If we want information, we must be willing to listen for it.

Think how much better off the management at NASA would have been had the supervisors at Morton Thiokol listened to the engineers who questioned the safety of the "O-rings" at certain temperatures on the Space Shuttle Challenger. They did not, and disaster resulted. While not all of our employees will have information this crucial in nature, it is better to have them say it to you before an accident or business problem occurs than after when you are picking up the pieces and trying to sort out what went wrong.

"THIS BETTER BE IMPORTANT"

One of the reasons people do not talk to us is that we simply do not have time for them. When they do come to talk with us, we communicate an attitude that says to them "this had better be important." As a result, employees come to realize that employers only want to listen on their own terms. This approach may seem operationally productive, but it catches up with employers during times of crisis or stress, not to mention in making long-term decisions that require employee involvement or input.

The only times the principal and superintendent come to eat with the employees at a small school district are when a) there is a crisis and they want to find out what people are thinking, or b) it is soon to be negotiating time, and they want employees to feel they are part of the family. A teacher from the school has a good laugh about this. Is this teacher a bit cynical? You bet, but for good reason. The only interaction is on the terms of those in power. Do those teachers feel like talking when the principal and superintendent show up? Of course not. These are such special occasions that the only things that get talked about are what the principal and superintendent want to hear, not really what is happening.

We are not advocating killing time through socializing at work, but you must create opportunities where your employees get a chance to interact with you. Peters and Austin (1985) call it "managing by walking around." You can call it what you want, but for people to want to talk to you, they have to believe that you will listen to them.

Contrary to popular management theory, employees don't magically begin to talk to you when you walk around. It is not a process of osmosis that occurs magically by "hanging out" with employees. It begins to happen when employees believe that you want to hear them, *really* hear them. It happens when they begin to see responses when they speak—in other words, you actually *are* listening. But remember, when they do finally begin to talk to you, you need to be ready to listen!

By finding time to listen, it communicates the attitude that you will always find the time to listen if employees have a concern. Too often interaction means talking. But to communicate a listening attitude you have to create it. An example of this is the owner of a manufacturing plant who occasionally rides with his truck drivers to deliver the product. Why waste a half day? For him, it gives the perfect chance to ask questions and listen to a group of employees who are often in the information loop. He doesn't waste a half day; he creates half-day opportunities to listen!

The executive director of a thriving nonprofit corporation finds the time to clean occasionally with his seasonal maintenance staff. The first time he did it, there were plenty of laughs. In fact, the cleaning staff wondered what he really was after. But after the second month, he began to find out what was really happening with the seasonal employees. Also, he began to find out why the seasonal employees had a strong dislike for a certain manager in the organization. That manager was wasteful and also dictatorial with the seasonal staff. It didn't take long for the executive director to realize that the perpetual personnel problem was not caused by the lower-level cleaning staff, but an inept manager who was manipulating the information.

'"No one likes to clean," he readily admits, "but it is one way to stay close to the employees and really get the inside track—not to mention the fact that after cleaning several hours, I have a much greater appreciation for what they do and for what I do."

You don't have to clean, and you don't have to ride with the delivery trucks, but somewhere down the line, you should make opportunities to listen. Quit hiding behind that excuse that there never is enough time! There is only time for what you feel is important. But realize that productivity, planning, and crisis management all begin with people. Knowing what is really happening with the people in your organization will have an impact both on your perspective and theirs. Uncomfortable to begin with, you bet! But worthwhile in the long run—you can count on it!

A GREAT WAY TO KILL LOYALTY

In Chapter 7 we talked about three types of filters—our experiences, how we apply those experiences to a situation, and our ego. These filters screen and reduce information at the point that we analyze and apply it to our understanding of the situation. In every organization there are human filters too. And, it doesn't take a brain surgeon to figure out who these people are in most organizations.

These human filters may include the secretarial staff, middle management, or members of the work team itself. Regardless of where they are, they have one thing in common: they know how to manipulate information so they look good. These human filters change the message as it gets passed along the line. Without realizing it, managers become human filters as well. That is, by changing what employees say to protect themselves, they manipulate the information that takes place. For example, managers with numerous employee problems may report none at all, so that their management style is not viewed as ineffective.

Soon after leaving college, Trent started working in a low-level staff position in a small company. As he observed the company, he came up with an idea of how to gain more capital funds for the organization. He went to the boss, Al, and submitted the plan in a four-page memo. Al liked the plan. But Trent never heard any more about it. That is, until two years later. At that point, Al and the board of directors approached Trent to take over a project that he and the chairperson of the board had for increasing capital funds for the organization. The project—you guessed it—was precisely the idea that Trent had submitted two years earlier.

Trent took the idea and ran with it. After all, success does not depend on who gets the credit for the idea; success often depends on who carries it out. But the bottom line was that Trent was never sure from that point on what information would get passed on as his (Trent's) and what information would get passed on as his boss's.

Because of the destruction of trust that occurs when a manager distorts something that is said for his own personal benefit, the filtering of information is one of the most critical failures in the creation of a listening environment. And whether it is done intentionally or unintentionally, it has the same effect.

In Chapters 6 and 7 we talked about the natural reduction and filtering of information that occurs as it passes through various channels within our mind and senses. The difference between reduction and filtering were also discussed. The main difference occurs because of control. Reduction is something that we cannot control. We can acknowledge it, but we cannot control it. Filtering, on the other hand, is something that managers can work to control. The point is that there need not be a breech of trust because of filtering. It *can* be controlled.

WHO DO I TALK TO?

At Corning Glassware, one of the changes that management brought about was designed to encourage communication. This was done by encouraging employee suggestions. But the change was not in just getting suggestions, the change included giving employees opportunities for having input into how the suggestions would be implemented. What is *even more significant* is the fact that employees are happier with that input than with receiving small checks for suggestions. If given a chance, employees do want to bring about positive changes for the company.

Everybody at some time or another wants to have a say in what is happening in their work life. Maybe they see a problem in the production line and don't feel good about turning out an inferior product. Maybe they know of a thief in the organization and wonder who they can tell. Maybe they are frustrated with how they are being treated by a supervisor. But what those employees want is some input into the decision-making process that controls their lives. What they often don't have is a vehicle to communicate with the people who make a difference in the organization.

Often it appears that management is at a loss as to what vehicles are available to listen to employees. In their writing, Peters and Austin repeatedly emphasize the importance of spending more time wandering around with your employees than sitting in an office. They emphasize the importance of informal moments of conversation which give real insight into the everyday problems that can occur both in productivity and product innovation.

There are numerous formal channels from which management can both communicate and listen to employees. These include: employee-management meetings, quality circles, newsletter question and answer columns, telephone lines, anonymously recording employee questions and concerns, suggestion systems, mentoring, coaching programs, and others. All of these suggestions are valid. It is important to remember that the size of the organization affects the number of vehicles that are needed to encourage and allow for employee communication. The key to remember is that one vehicle is not enough. It is a nice theory to think that simply by walking around, or riding with drivers, or even cleaning with employees, you can create the atmosphere for listening. The fact is that one communication vehicle is probably not enough—particularly for growing organizations.

The best way to encourage listening so that people will speak is to provide multiple channels for interaction. Once again, unless management has been trained and is motivated to listen, no program will be effective. Effective listening skills allow—open up the channels—for a variety of voices to be heard through a variety of means.

Listening to employees can be a key to innovation and growth. Management must listen so that employees will *want* to speak. They must demonstrate ongoing, positive listening behaviors that reinforce the desire not only to hear what is said, but use and respond to speaking employees—the "active listening" process.

TEST YOUR UNDERSTANDING

Ask yourself these five questions as you seek to overcome the barriers to effective listening:

1) Are you receiving all the information you can?
2) Do you create time for others to talk with you?
3) Are you distorting the information you get because of filters?
   a. Do you have strong, personal biases that interfere?
   b. Are you one who is quick to judge and evaluate others?
   c. Are you willing to hear another person out despite the way they look or talk?
   d. Are you generally secure, self-confident, and extroverted so that you are not threatened by information others give you?
   e. Are you one who needs the information of others to do the best you can?
4) Do employees know who they can go to if they want to talk? Do they know the channels that are available?

PART FIVE

How Can Managers Listen So Supervisors Will Speak?

CHAPTER 18

What Is Your Key To Upward Mobility?

"The role of the supervisor is to make certain that the behaviors of subordinates are compatible with the interest of the organization. This role is most easily performed when a strong, positive relationship exists between the supervisor and subordinates." This quotation was part of an academic study done on supervisors by Richmond, McCroskey and Davis in 1986 and underscores the importance of the supervisor to the survival of a business.

But what is it that underscores, or helps assure, the "strong, positive relationship" that needs to exist? To be successful, every management team member and every employee must listen so that their supervisors will speak.

This is an odd way to think about this "strong, positive relationship." Supervisors are just naturally supposed to speak and give responsibilities to subordinates. One does not normally think that the approach to listening has anything to do with the amount of speaking or the types of information that will be shared by the supervisor. Yet subordinate listening abilities have *everything* to do with getting a job, getting promoted, and then keeping a management-level position.

As discussed earlier, one study noted that effective listening was one of the keys to upward mobility (Sypher, Bostrom and Seibert 1989). The authors of this study wrote, "What we can conclude from this study is that listening is related to other communication abilities and to success at work. Better listeners held higher-level positions and were promoted more often than those with less-developed listening abilities." This was a very significant finding.

When 1,000 personnel managers were asked to list the top two skills most important for getting a job—the same study we cited in Chapter 9 (Curtis, Winsor and Stephens, 1989)—they said oral communication and listening. The top two skills important for successful job performance, interpersonal or human relations skills and oral communication skills, both involve effective listening. An ideal management profile for an on-the-job-manager focused on skills that demand good listening abilities: the ability to work well with others one-on-one, the ability to gather accurate information from others to make a decision, the ability to work well in small groups, and the ability to listen effectively and give counsel. While only one of these skills mentions listening, all of the skills interrelate directly with listening abilities. As mentioned in Chapter 10, in 25 different studies focusing on critical employment skills, the one skill mentioned most often was listening (Sypher, Bostrom and Seibert, 1989).

How one listens impacts on how one will succeed in a company. Think for just a moment, do employees' successes depend on fulfilling what their supervisors expect? If you ignore what your supervisor wants, you aren't going to be around very long. Regardless whether your supervisor is one person, a board of directors, or a large group of shareholders, your success is linked to fulfilling expectations and desires. If your leadership doesn't express what their expectations are, you are in a position to fail.

We were in a seminar several years ago when the presenter said, "The No. 1 complaint of American workers today is that they do not know what is expected." Common sense would tell you that employees have to know what is expected to be successful in their jobs. You would think this is obvious, but what seems like common sense is not always common knowledge. Leadership may not tell you what they expect. They may *assume* that you know.

If you do not know what is expected, it is their fault for not telling you, right? Yes, it may be their fault that you failed, but try to explain that as you go to get your next job or negotiate for a higher salary. The bottom line is that regardless of whose fault it is, performance depends on direction, and direction comes from your ability to know and understand what leadership demands. That's what the words "initiative," "insight," "enterprise," "ambition," and "wisdom" are all about. These are all traits of high-quality leadership. And these traits are also what merit and promotion often depend upon.

Let's use an analogy here. Being successful in a job is like giving gifts to others, especially significant others. Unless you learn what the other person likes, you are not likely to give gifts that please. We remember learning about Jackie Joyner-Kersee, sometimes referred to as the world's greatest female athlete. When she won the gold medal in the 1992 Summer Olympics, her husband and trainer gave her a dozen roses—forgetting that Jackie does not like roses. He admitted in an interview that he made a mistake. He was the one who likes flowers, not her. He was giving Jackie a gift that pleased him, not her, and her negative reaction was recorded for the world to see.

When we do not learn what others like, we may give them gifts that please us and not them. To really give a special gift, it has to be something that will please *them.* In the same way, to be successful on the job, your energies have to please your supervisor—whether *you* like it or not.

It is easy to assign this concept of "listening so that your supervisor will speak" to someone else, for example, the line worker or clerical worker. But consider this: *The Wall Street Journal* ran a story about a major utilities company battling back from a take-over attempt. The CEO repeatedly said that what he underestimated in the management of the company was that if the company was profitable and he did a good job, the shareholders would support him. What he did not realize was that until management's expectations matched those of his shareholders, he was in jeopardy of losing the company. He went on to say that he fought off the takeover by making sure that his shareholders knew he was listening and sensitive to their wants, needs, and desires. He now spends large amounts of time traveling—traveling to listen to major shareholders as a means of keeping the company in tune with its future, in tune with the future that investors view as important. This CEO learned that you listen not only for what expectations are, but listening helps you *anticipate* what the needs will be. Listening to others' expectations was and is critical to his success.

In another example, there is a chairman of a large conglomerate who swore to communication consultants hired to conduct a communication audit that "everybody" in the corporation shared his vision of the company's future. He was so convinced he said, "Talk to some people. You won't find any surprises."

James H. Foster, president of Brouillard Communications, who did the communication audit, wrote "We found a lot of surprises" (Eisenhart 1989). Is this typical? You bet. Can the problem be remedied? Of course.

Here was a chairman of a corporation who assumed everyone was listening and in agreement with him. Obviously he was wrong! Now, was it the chairman's fault that he did not know the true beliefs of his people, or was it the subordinates' fault?

We have been talking about the role of the chairman, supervisor, leader, or manager in the listening process. The chairman clearly did not have good listening channels established and was out of touch with his subordinates. But remember that listening is a process; it is not an isolated episode.

Employees practicing good listening skills must respond! In the case of the supervisor out of touch with his constituency, the employees may have chosen *not* to respond with honest feedback. In this situation, the integrity of both the listening and speaking is in question. Obviously, the chairman thought he had communicated, yet the response to his message informed him of the discrepancies in his opinion. The chairman may not have been listening to the responses, or the employees may have withheld an important part of the listening process—honest feedback.

This is why establishing an effective listening environment is important. It shows that those in charge care, and because they care, it is more likely that subordinates will respond. The key is that communication is a two-way process that involves *both* speaking and listening. Employees need to recognize this as well as supervisors.

Answering the question that forms the title of the chapter, "What is Your Key to Upward Mobility?" the answer should now be clear. What is it that underscores, or helps assure, the "strong, positive relationship" that must exist between management and employees? To be successful, every management team member and every employee must listen so supervisors will speak. Employees also need to be willing to respond with feedback so that open, available, accurate information can flow up the corporate ladder as well as down.

CHAPTER 19

How Do You Discover What Your Supervisor Thinks Is Important?

Monty Frisco said, "The key to seduction is not found in what you say, it is found in the questions you ask. It is not in what you talk about, but in what you listen for. The right questions combined with a listening ear are the only tools you need for this journey of allurement." To be seductive, according to Monty Frisco involves asking the right questions and having a listening ear.

You might wonder what this has to do with discovering what your supervisor thinks is important? The discovery process begins like Monty Frisco's description of seduction. It starts with learning how to ask the right questions and then learning how to listen to the response. Most people want to convince their supervisors or their constituents, or their shareholders that they know what is important. They do this by telling their supervisors (or constituents or shareholders) what *they* think is important—as if somehow by expounding on what they value, the message is transferred into the minds and values of others.

Even in selling an idea, selling isn't telling, it's *asking.*

The problem is that it is like the dating process. I convince you how lucky you are to be going out with me by telling you how good I am. But eventually you realize that I am more interested in telling you how good I am than in having a relationship. Consequently those involved stop talking.

When people stop talking and look for ways to avoid, ignore, or worse yet, get rid of the other person, the relationship is doomed to failure. The point is that you have to stop talking about what *you* value, and learn to ask what it is that the other person values. You have to frame your concerns in the form of a question, and then listen for the response. When you talk, make your comments brief, provide options, and get to the point. Showing a relationship partner that you care doesn't mean telling, it means asking.

ASKING QUESTIONS

Remember, most everyone wants to talk, but discovering what your supervisor thinks is important is a matter of asking the right questions. Supervisors are concerned with time—yours and theirs. Asking a question assumes that a) you want an answer, and b) that you will do something with the answer you have been given. You should avoid asking questions unless these two points hold true.

Sensitivity to their response to any question you ask is important. Even if you choose not to follow up exactly with a response that is in keeping with their answer to your question, remember that their response gives you a point of reference from which you can draw. For example, you ask a supervisor, "What is the exact deadline for the full report?" Let's suppose the supervisor says, "The final deadline is exactly one month from today, but *your* deadline is in just two weeks." You may not follow up with a response that is in keeping with the supervisor's statement. You might say, for example, "We have a number of outside consultants working on the project," which is only remotely connected to his last statement.

But his statement offers a point of reference, the comment about "just two weeks," from which you can draw. For example, you might say, "Yes, this will be a busy two weeks," to let him know that you are aware of *your* deadline. This is the "engage in paraphrasing" portion of the H.E.A.R. method of listening. Also, you could follow up with a second question, "Do you know who gets the report first in two weeks?" The point is that by listening to his response to your question, you get a point of reference that will help you in steering the process.

Let's back up for a minute. What is your motivation for asking the question in the first place? If you want to know what is important to your supervisor on a particular project or task, remember that the way he or she responds will be linked to the timing and phrasing of the question. In the above situation, it looks like making the deadline is important to the supervisor. But the best way we have to discover what is most important is by creating the proper environment so that this answer can be given.

Mark is an employee who chooses the company staff meeting to ask specific questions about his job. He does it to make a point rather than to get an answer. Once when Mark did this, he put the president of the company on the spot. The president's response to Mark was aimed more at diplomacy than forthrightness about the issue.

Later, whenever Mark would come to the president of the company with a question, the president would weigh Mark's words carefully, because he never knew whether he might choose a public forum later to make a related point. That seemed to be Mark's normal way of operating—using a public forum to air specific concerns.

The lesson here is, if you want a straight answer, you need to carefully and wisely choose when to ask questions. Asking questions tells supervisors what you are thinking. Along with the questions, your credibility and competence (or lack of credibility and incompetence) are closely attached. The timing of the questions and the way the questions are asked are as important as the content of what is being asked.

Merle, for example, was embarrassed when he asked the president of his company if he had just spoken to shareholders when he was coming out of the building where shareholder meetings are normally held. It was actually a stupid question because Merle was off by one week. The shareholders meeting was next week. It made Merle feel like a fool once he discovered his error.

Also, questions should not be used to grind a point home or to trap another employee or a supervisor. When this is done, often it comes back to haunt the person asking the question. Jeffrey, for example, one time asked if both Staci and Bill had been consulted before a decision to go ahead with the project had been made. Jeffrey knew ahead of time that there was a vicious power struggle between Staci and Bill and it was unlikely both would have been consulted about the project. Jeffrey asked the question to bring the power struggle out in the open. It was a thoughtless idea.

When other employees realize that another employee is using his or her questions in staff meetings to manipulate or to reveal weaknesses, or irrelevant problems, the tables will quickly get turned. The next time this employee makes a mistake, the types of questions that come up in the staff meeting are likely to emphasize and even exaggerate this mistake. Jeffrey had stationery ordered that included wrong information and this mistake cost the company a bundle.

Because of his previous question about Staci and Bill, when budget cutting was mentioned someone asked "Is someone planning to control Jeffrey's budget?" What goes around comes around!

If you do ask a question, but you interrupt to make your own point or to answer your own question, you have damaged your opportunities for encouraging a supervisor to speak—both now and in the future. Questions are for listening and learning, both for others and for you. There is no need to grind points home. Supervisors can learn about your competence through your ability to frame excellent, intelligent questions. They can learn about your people skills by observing your ability to keep your mouth shut long enough to carefully listen to the answers to your questions.

Most all types of business is based on salesmanship. Even listening so that supervisors will speak is based on the listener's ability to sell himself or herself. Look what Rich Goldman, senior vice president and general sales manager of Television Program Enterprises, a division of Cox Enterprises, has to say about the importance of both asking questions and listening in sales:

"Without questions, the sales process can fall apart before it begins. When I hire salespeople, I always ask them what they feel are the characteristics of a good salesperson. The one answer I look for more than any other is the ability to be a good listener. By inference that suggests they are asking questions."

USE MULTIPLE CHANNELS OF COMMUNICATION

In Chapter 17 we talked about the importance of multiple channels of communication for employees to speak with supervisors. The same holds true when employees want to create an atmosphere for supervisors to speak. If we want constituents to speak with politicians or shareholders to speak to CEOs, the same holds true. In the office, this means that as an employee you create multiple means of interaction with your supervisor.

You let supervisors know, for example, that you value their counsel by not wasting their time. So when issues are minor, you frame them as being minor in a memo, where supervisors can respond briefly on the same sheet. For example, you might say, "Although this is a minor issue, I would like to include Elaine in our meeting Friday. She has special expertise in this area. If you agree, let me know, and

I will invite her." Another option is to send the memo through the computer and frame it as minor by giving supervisors several options from which they can choose for their response.

Stating the issue briefly and then framing the solution with what you see as being potential options, tells supervisors that you are thinking. For example, you could say, "Several ideas for new projects have crossed my desk recently. I would like to discuss them with you. If you are available, we could talk just before lunch in your office tomorrow. If that won't work, perhaps I could drop by your office at 5:30 when we would have a few minutes to talk. A third possibility is the first thing Thursday morning. I think you will find these ideas promising." Memos like the one above brings supervisors up to speed as to what you think are the available options. But, most importantly, it gives them a response point. They can choose or reject any option if you frame it in a way that allows them freedom of action. Here again, you want to listen to them, so even by giving them what you think are the most important options, you need to encourage a response that may or may not conform to your choice.

When issues are major, you need to personally and privately give the question to them directly. Choose the time and place wisely. For example, in the memo above, it was always the supervisor's office where the meeting was to take place. This was an important choice because the memo writer wanted the supervisor's honest reactions to business-related ideas that might require the supervisor to use notes, figures, or other material he knew she had in her office.

In memos it is also a good idea to offer at least some starting point in your perception of the problem or in your presentation of ideas. For example, "There has been a problem with the quality of some of the parts we are getting. Perhaps you are aware of it. I would like to discuss with you the possibility of finding some other suppliers." This allows supervisors to think about your question (or memo) from the perspective of possible solutions as well as giving them the advantage of as much information as possible.

In raising questions, presenting issues, or pointing out problems, the main point is that you want to give supervisors the freedom to reject all options in favor of a new approach or suggestion they might have. This maintains the proper respect for position, regard for authority, and consideration for accountability. More important, it keeps the channels of communication open. It is a way to listen so that supervisors will speak.

What is important is that you have multiple channels of communication with supervisors, constituents, and shareholders. You could, for example, use the phone, visit in person, write a memo, use the computer, take time out for lunch, or take them out to breakfast. Whatever you do, remember multiple approaches gives them many opportunities to speak and also gives you plenty of opportunities to listen. Of course, you can't do all of this in a week! It takes time and energy.

You will probably have to adjust your schedule to fit what is best for supervisors, constituents, and shareholders. You should remain flexible and be spontaneous in responding to their needs, times, or responses. Often they are not nearly as flexible or adaptable as you might wish. But in the long run, if you develop multiple channels, ask intelligent questions, and listen for their responses, they will speak, and when they do—under these conditions—it will be best for you.

How do you discover what your supervisor thinks is important? You choose the right time to ask good questions. Then you carefully and sensitively listen to the answers. You let the supervisor's answer target your next question or response. In this way, the supervisor frames the direction of the conversation, and you take your direction and focus from him or her.

Questions are a great confidence builder because we are at our most competitive and we are our most effective when we work from a base of knowledge. Can you imagine going to a doctor or to a lawyer who didn't ask you any questions? Questions are at the core of discovering what is important.

CHAPTER 20

Why Listen When No One Expects You To?

Information is power. Having the right information at the right time can mean the difference between success and failure. Getting the right information often means learning to listen when it is unexpected. Since most of us listen selectively, we listen simply to things that interest us. For example, think of the last time you went to dinner with several other people. They began talking about a subject that was unfamiliar or uninteresting to you. Your natural tendency was to allow your mind to wander. Or, you are sitting in a staff meeting and a member of another department is raising an issue with the boss that does not concern your department. Your natural tendency, once again, is to either engage someone else in discussion or to simply think of other things—to let your mind wander.

If information is power, then the more you understand the people and the organization, the better positioned you will be to succeed. What we are suggesting is that you listen and catalogue information even when it is *not* a requirement. It's not enough to listen, you must listen and then act. You need to begin a notebook, index cards, or something that records important pieces of information. Information such as: when birthdays are, hobbies enjoyed by coworkers and the boss, names of spouses and children, important past and present company problems, company legends and stories, and so on. The list could go on and on. However, one does not know when or how the information could be useful in the future. The only way to remember is to write things down. To record it is to remember it for the future.

When you listen and learn, you will find yourself developing common ground faster because you understand the context of important and significant events. You will be able to initiate more productive conversations because you can begin with something that links information to another person's interests. When you have to make a presentation to the boss, you will be able to frame the presentation in a way that indicates you have a grasp on past problems and, consequently, you will not be prone to fall into the similar traps.

Listening unexpectedly means just that—listening for things that no one expects you to remember. Several years ago Louis was trying to gain the support of an important investor and CEO by the name of Clifford McKenzie. As Louis came into McKenzie's office for a meeting, McKenzie was finishing up another meeting with George, his production manager. They were discussing an organizational problem and how they should deal with it. As Louis sat down, they continued to discuss it and, after George left, McKenzie complained to Louis about the problem. He ended this by saying, "Well, enough about my problems, what can I do for you?"

McKenzie did not expect Louis to listen to his problems because in his mind, McKenzie felt Louis was there for his own agenda. McKenzie and Louis talked and Louis left. After he left he wrote down what he had heard in the discussion between McKenzie and George.

Two weeks later, as Louis was going through a trade publication, he happened upon a lead article that was on the very problem discussed by McKenzie and George, the production manager. Before Louis and the CEO met again Louis sent the article to him with a note saying that he remembered the issue that McKenzie had been struggling with and thought that the article might be of interest.

Guess what the first topic for discussion was the next time Louis and McKenzie happened to be together? You guessed it. The article and the problem. When McKenzie finally got around to Louis's agenda, he was ready to listen. Why? Because he knew that Louis valued the things that he valued. That gave Louis and McKenzie common ground or a means of identification. It also gave Louis the influence he needed to gain McKenzie's support. Information means influence. Listen, learn, and write it down. Sooner or later, you are likely to be the one with the *right information* and that is something people tend to remember. Listen when it is not expected because it can provide some interesting as well as influential information. One teacher we know instructs her students to be "sponges for knowledge," and this is similar to what we are advocating here.

What can you listen for? Listen for:

- problems
- birthdays
- names of children, spouses, key employees
- future trends
- future problems
- ideas
- hobbies and interests
- educational background

In addition to the above, you can listen to people who often are not heard. Listen, for example, to:

- secretaries
- custodians
- cleaning people
- customers
- colleagues
- family members
- rivals and competitors
- employees of other companies
- suppliers or venders
- relationship partners
- friends

PART SIX

HOW CAN MANAGERS FIND THE "TRIP WIRES?"

CHAPTER 21

How Can You Use Trip Wires To Increase Effectiveness?

You have an innovative idea that you think is both good for the company and potentially good for your career. You happen to see the boss, and you run the idea past him, and he explodes. He says to you, "That idea is not in your job description, and it is not something that I have time to consider! Focus on doing your own work," he continues, "Let someone in R&D deal with the innovative stuff."

So what happened? Your idea was blown to pieces without you being given a chance to explain it. Was it something you said? Was the boss just having a bad day? What was it that caused you to lose a potentially good idea, and seemed to trigger a minor explosion?

Communication "trip wires" are something we all have. They can be tripped when we least expect it. Someone says something that just seems to set you off. Or you say something, as in the above example, and the other person flies off the handle.

If you don't think you have communication "trip wires," think back to the last time you were with your parents. Suddenly, you seemed to change from being an adult to being a "son" or a "daughter" when talking to mom or dad. Now, think for a minute about your last conflict at their home. Was it the subject that set you off? Was it the way it was said? Or, was it the role *you* were assuming?

Don has a grandfather who is an alcoholic and any reference to alcoholism or drinking tends to set him off. Barbara's "trip wire" is strong language used in her presence. Frederick has always had difficulty with the way his father talks to him. Melanie hates to get into political discussions. Regardless what the issue is or how it is triggered, something in the past probably acted like a trip wire that caused you to immediately react. In a different context, it might not have bothered you, but at home with your parents, it bugs you, and you react.

Remember, when you detect someone's trip wire, you can either be blown to bits or you can use that knowledge to deal more effectively with that person. What is a *trip wire?* Something that causes someone to immediately respond or react in a way that is not planned or thought out. The trip wire may be an issue, like some of those mentioned earlier. For some people, issues such as AIDS, abortion, rape, feminine or minority rights, incompetence, or welfare cause an immediate reaction.

In other instances, the trip wire may be a person such as a co-worker who drives you crazy or a boss who always seems to be on your case. The trip wire may be a situation like standing in line for a long time or not finding a parking place when you are in a hurry. Trip wires come in a variety of forms, but they all have one thing in common: they provoke a communication response that is not thought out and is uncontrolled.

It is this lack of thinking and control that makes it easy to control someone if you understand what pushes their buttons or trips their wire. We can control the fire when we trip the wire! In Chapter 25 we discuss listening to yourself so you can control your emotions. We also discuss developing habits of self-control and learning positive self-talk to maintain emotional control. But the fact is, everyone does not exercise self-control. And if you do not understand the concept of trip wires, or if you do not understand how to use them, you risk becoming a casualty of someone else's lack of self-control! It is tempting to see this as manipulation. If you know what sets someone off, you manipulate the person to get the response you want at the time you want it. "Don't see Charlie now; he's in a terrible mood!" How and when trip wires are used also has some ethical implications. The point of finding and understanding trip wires is not to manipulate, but to avoid being a casualty.

Kids are fabulous for detecting and using trip wires. Early in their lives, they discover that a scene in a public place will get them anything they want. They know public scenes are embarrassing to parents; public scenes are trip wires. They spend twelve years developing a map that locates parents' trip wires. Then, when they become a teenager, they bring out the map. They realize parents value a clean car, so they make a clean car a bargaining chip for using it for a date.

They learn which parent to approach about what subject. For example, they discover dad is a soft touch for getting more money. But mom is the one to go to for extending curfew or for getting out of chores. They know how to use trip wires to play one parent off the other. "I just talked to mom," Maggie says to her dad, "And she says its okay that all my friends and I go to Florida over the break." They may know that when company comes over is the time to raise the point about how the car was scratched "by accident" this morning on the way to school or that they need some additional allowance. The company nervously smiles. What the teenagers may fail to mention is how the parents had to call six times to get them out of bed this morning, and they left the house late for school. Or they may fail to mention that the allowances have been raised twice during the last month or that a big purchase was made using up all of their allowance for three months! With company over, the map tells the teenagers that their own trip wires will not be triggered while it is safe to trigger their parents' trip wires!

To use trip wires to your advantage, you have to know two things. First, you have to know what the trip wires are, and, second, you have to know what sets them off. How does this relate to listening? You cannot learn what your boss's (or anyone else's) trip wires are without listening. You cannot learn when it is to your advantage to trip a reaction, and when it is to your advantage not to trip a reaction, if you have not learned how to listen.

When it comes to making trip-wire decisions, good judgment must be intertwined with listening. If you want to avoid the explosion, you listen for what causes the explosion. For example, early in their marriage Edward and Karen got into some heated arguments about things they did before they were married. For both, these events were trip wires. So, to help preserve harmony in their marriage, they agreed never to bring up things that happened before their marriage. For Edward and Karen, this worked successfully to help them avoid those heated arguments and discussions. For them, this trip-wire decision, based on the good judgment they showed from listening to each other, probably helped keep their marriage together.

But trip wires are more than simply learning about explosions. They are also about learning to listen for what trips negative and positive responses. By learning about what trips the response, you learn how to frame the issue. For example, your supervisor, Harold, made it clear one day that he did not want to hear what the competition was doing. His focus was *his* company, *not* his competition. But you heard that the competition had made a move that could seriously affect the well-being of your company, and you thought it was important that Harold know about it. What you chose to do was to frame it so that Harold would think of it as just a new idea or a unique suggestion, rather than "what the competition" was doing. By listening, you learned how to frame the issue in such a way that Harold would respond, not explode.

Context, past experiences, and the link between time and the emotions are three powerful trip wires. Often these trip wires are easy to identify and are easy to use to your advantage. In the next three chapters, we will look at these three powerful trip wires.

CHAPTER 22

How Can You Find A Trip Wire In Context?

A pep rally demands a certain kind of motivational speech. A funeral oration requires a certain reverence. And a business address before shareholders has its own set of demands, restrictions, and characteristics. Context dictates the kind of speech that is appropriate. Trip wires, too, are related to context.

The context often dictates the response. Everyone is concerned about saving face. Everyone is concerned about how he or she appears to others. Good negotiators understand this better than anyone. They want to choose the context where negotiation is to take place.

Remember the Vietnam Peace Talks? Those representing the various countries involved argued for weeks just on *how* the room would be arranged and how the table would be shaped. Even at the Middle East Peace talks that started in 1991, the talks almost broke down because the sides could not come to agreement on where the talks would be held. In both situations, the individuals involved understood the importance of context to communication.

But let's examine the issue of context on a specific, practical basis. Think about the communication that takes place in your office. When people are present, the boss may give a totally different response from the one given if it were just the two of you. Coming to talk to you in your office might prompt a different response when compared with you going to his or her office. The context for where the communication takes place often dictates whether you will be able to create an atmosphere where listening is most likely to occur.

If you want to understand how context is a trip wire in your organization, listen! Where, for example, does it seem that your boss (if that is the person you are targeting) is likely to talk freely with you or with others? Is it in your office? Is it in his or her office? When no one else is around? Is it when you are out to lunch at a favorite restaurant? We need to capitalize on the location. For example, Jerome found that Suzanne, his boss, would *only* discuss business in *her* office. Outside of that office, it was far more social conversation than business. If people wanted to discuss business, they knew precisely where this was to be done.

Context is important. When you discover where people are most comfortable discussing certain issues, you will want to make certain to follow the "rules" that you discover. For example, we knew one department chair who would never "talk shop" when socializing. If it ever happened, he would very politely and very gently say something like, "That is an important idea. Let's take that up at work tomorrow." His point was clear.

If you want a person to speak so that you can listen, then you need to make the context a critical issue. If talking shop is confined to the office, then that is the place where you can ask questions that require a wider-scale response. If talking on a social basis is confined to lunches, picnics, and celebrations, then that is where you become a "sponge for knowledge" and listen for the information we outlined in Chapter 20.

There is another aspect of context that needs to concern listeners. Where does your boss seem least likely to speak freely, or where is he or she likely to act abruptly? This is the place where you give bullets of information. This is the place where you only ask questions that require a limited response. This is the place where time is crucial so questions and responses must be succinct—capsulized.

Location is a critical trip wire for creating an atmosphere where people will speak. A negative response, a quick brush off, or an abrupt, almost hostile, comment that you receive may not be an accurate response at all. Of course, it could be. But it could be a response to the context and not to the idea. Effective listeners are sensitive to when and where conversations take place if good, solid information is desired. Context can dictate communication.

CHAPTER 23

How Can You Use Past Experiences As Positive Trip Wires?

When Dennis was brought in as the president, Hal knew it was a good choice. Hal knew that Dennis received his business degree from the University of Michigan. Hal also knew that Dennis had been born and raised in Michigan. And Hal knew that Dennis's rise in the business had been very similar to his own.

As it turned out, everything Hal knew about Dennis's background, education, and interests was borne out. Not only did Hal and Dennis become best of friends because of these similarities, but Hal quickly became one of Dennis's closest confidants and advisors. Hal knew how to use past experience as an effective, positive trip wire that benefited Dennis, the business, and, of course, Hal.

Past experiences are trip wires that evoke a response because of our filters and our tendency toward reducing information. The key is to listen to find out as much as possible about others' past experiences and frames of reference.

If your boss is the target, to whom do you listen to gain this trip-wire advantage? Listening to other supervisors talk about your boss, listening to the boss's supervisor, and listening to co-workers provides insight into what your boss has gone through to get to this point in his or her career.

It is only through understanding the past that we can begin to predict the future. Consequently, learning about your boss's failures and successes enables you to tailor comments to trip a response that is connected to a past success rather than a failure. You can direct more effectively and control your communication to get the desired results.

Several years ago Glenn was raising money so that a nonprofit corporation could purchase some land adjoining the corporation's property. Glenn knew it was going to be a difficult sales job in the small, rural community where he was going to visit. Glenn lined up a lunch meeting with a group of local businessmen from this rural town.

Prior to the meeting, he asked for background information on the people who would be attending. Glenn's contact talked to him about the various people, but he highlighted one influential member of the group and community, Walter Olmstead, who the contact thought was opposed to the purchase. Walter's support was necessary if the purchase was to occur. If Walter was negative or silent, all efforts to gain support in that community would be difficult, if not impossible, the contact told Glenn.

Several days before the meeting, Glenn asked questions and listened to anyone who could talk about the past successes and failures of Walter Olmstead. Walter became the focus, the preoccupation, the very center of Glenn's thinking, for several weeks. Glenn learned, for example, that many years ago Walter was heading up a visionary future project for this same nonprofit corporation. At that time, few people supported the project. And, while the visionary future project received very poor support, years later the project was proving to be a tremendous success. This was not just a useful piece of information, it could be crucial to Glenn's success or failure.

The lunch meeting came and Walter Olmstead was present. Glenn made his pitch. He reached the end of the presentation, looked directly at Walter and said, "Walter, years ago you had an idea similar to this one. It concerned a land purchase, and people did not have the vision at that time to see how important it would be. Yet today, we know that decision proved to be successful beyond anyone's dreams or imagination. Now," Glenn continued, "we are faced with a similar long-term need that demands vision. What do you think?"

After pausing a moment, almost like a salesperson making a close, Walter turned to the group as a whole, and he talked about the idea from years ago and how people didn't support it. He talked about how he knew it was the right thing to do. The minute Walter started talking about the past visionary project he had been involved in, Glenn knew that eventually he would get his support.

Glenn's homework was obvious. Because he spent time investigating Walter's background, and because he indicated, by the time he took, how important this decision was to him, Glenn increased his credibility—what Walter and the group thought of him—and thus his potential success. In this case, all Glenn's work paid off.

Glenn knew that he could not control the contextual setting. That was predetermined but, because it was held in Walter's small, rural town, the setting actually favored the businessmen. It was not neutral. What Glenn *could* control was the trip wire that dealt with Walter's past experiences. To get his support, Walter had to link Glenn's idea with one in his *own* past—one that had been a success. It was that linkage with success that helped determine Glenn's own success.

While we do not suggest manipulating bosses or supervisors, we do suggest that there are possibilities for linking our ideas and experiences with their past ideas and experiences. If we want to avoid negative trip wires, if we want to avoid those we are trying to persuade from going silent on us, if we want to make sure that common ground (identification) is working for us and not against us, then we have to learn what trips them up. We need to learn to listen for past experiential trip wires, both positive and negative, and then we need to neatly weave them into our presentation. In this way, we can use trip wires to our advantage.

CHAPTER 24

How Can You Use Emotions And Time As Trip Wires?

Beth always arrived at work about forty-five minutes before anyone else. She loved the solitude. It was during this time that she did not want to be bothered. She used the time to plan her day, to establish her priorities, and to make certain the loose ends from the day before were tied up. Because Beth depended on and protected this time as if it was sacred, you can imagine how emotional she got if the time were interfered with in any way. This was one time when everyone knew that Beth was unavailable.

Emotions and time are the two trip wires that are linked to each other. The person who said, "Don't put off until tomorrow, what you can do today," didn't think about how time and the emotions can affect both decisions and how willing people are to speak openly.

Both men and women have *that* time of the day, *that* time of the week, *that* time of the month, and *that* time of the year when their emotions can be tripped more easily. We know Andrew, who is a teacher, operates at a fever pitch during the academic year. At that time, he is more emotional. During summers, he is more relaxed, able to think, respond, and make decisions more casually, rationally, and comfortably. This is when Andrew does all his writing, his planning for the academic year, and most of his thinking about professional needs and concerns. Things race during the academic year; things are more relaxed and appropriately paced during summers when his emotions are not stretched to their limits. Obviously we're not talking here simply about biological problems, although it certainly could be biological for both men and women as well as preference.

We all have peak periods during the day when we simply do not want or like interruptions—just like Beth. For us, that time is in the morning. We hate to be interrupted in the morning. It is our peak creative time. We ease off somewhat after lunch, and we are in the mood to deal with people more in the afternoon than any other time. Why is that? It is probably a combination of both preference and practice.

Most everybody has periods or seasons where time is at a premium and occasions where there is time for others. The trick is learning to connect those times with your schedule. We need to find others' preferences and zero in on them. We need to make semi-regular appointments with people at this time of the day. Of course, we should not do so unless we have something to talk about. Nobody wants their time wasted. Also, we should not do this if we are going to do all the talking. It is useful and important to find a valid and justifiable reason to listen to supervisors during these special times, and to do it semi-regularly.

Why semi-regularly? Norman was attempting to get Mitchell Osborn, a company president, to invest in his organization. He wanted and needed his support both from a financial perspective and from a knowledge and experience perspective. Mitchell had a wealth of knowledge and experience which had brought him and his company remarkable success. Norman knew this. What Mitchell would be able to share with Norman's organization about the market they were trying to penetrate for investment capital was worth just as much as any capital he was willing to invest. Norman learned that Mitchell's schedule was packed. Mitchell started as an early riser, and the one time during the day that he had free was breakfast.

As much as Norman hated to get up early, every meeting that he set up with Mitchell was for early breakfast. Norman actually learned to enjoy breakfast at Mitchell's hour. At that time, Mitchell was typically relaxed; there were no interruptions that early, and he was in the mood to talk. Everyone else seemed to want to talk to him during the day, but breakfast was one time when he could talk and Norman would listen.

Norman made a point to meet with him semi-regularly—once a month or once every other month. The emotions come into play when a meeting is simply a one-time event. The trip wire you get is the emotion that people are experiencing at that moment. They may react with impatience, not because of your idea, but because they just remembered that their anniversary is today and they did not acknowledge it this morning to their spouse.

The problem is that when meetings are one-time events, you cannot predict what emotion may be predominant at the moment. Consequently if the person with whom you are meeting is someone important to you—a boss or an important client—you need that semi-regular meeting at their best time to balance out the unpredictables. Meeting semi-regularly allows you to realize that because the boss is impatient or upset today, does not mean the emotional trip wire was you, your idea, or your attitude.

Doug Riggs is the CEO of a small water-treatment company. Doug makes certain that all of his salespeople make semi-regular calls on the company's clients, whether they require a call or not. In this way, the sales staff can make notes on how the water treatment chemicals are working, possible future needs of the clients, and any changes in staff, chemical needs, or machinery. These calls are important as a public relations arm of this small company, and Doug builds his business through his continuing concern for his clients. Also, he can better make use of emotions and time in sales presentations because he knows his clients so well—their emotions and their time restrictions.

Time is a trip wire that can be used in your favor as well. When Norman met Mitchell, Norman made it clear he was not there to hard sell Mitchell on his own organization. He made it clear that he honestly wanted his feedback and his ideas. As a result, trust was built. As a result, Mitchell became more interested in Norman's life. As a result, Mitchell felt free to speak and respond, as did Norman. Consequently when Norman needed to talk to Mitchell at other less convenient times, Mitchell was willing to talk. Why? Because the time trip wire was associated with the positive morning meetings, so less convenient times were not instantly seen as negative.

PART SEVEN

How Can Managers Listen
To Cope With Conflict?

CHAPTER 25

How Can You Listen To Yourself To Control Your Emotions?

For many people, their emotions get in their way. All of us were born with the capacity for tremendous emotions. Fortunately most of them are healthy. But none of us were given the knowledge of how to deal with them. This we all learn for ourselves.

A former brother-in-law of one of the authors was a victim of his emotions. In many different situations, he would look for words, phrases, or events that would trigger his emotions, and then, for what seemed like no apparent reason, he would strike out. For what seemed like either no cause or such a little cause, he would overreact. He would behave in ways that caused problems—simply because he had not learned to control his emotions.

Many of us, we're sure, have experienced times when we *knew* that it would be better to remain calm and in control of ourselves only to discover that our emotions took over anyway. Why does this happen? What can be done to control our emotions?

First, we need to recognize the *Emotional Cycle. (See Figure 25.1.)* This figure is composed of situation, thought, chemical response, emotions created, more thoughts created; and the cycle repeats itself, building the emotional response as it repeats. Many of us go through this cycle, sometimes many times during the day, and often it occurs without us knowing it. It works like this:

1. A situation occurs that is upsetting.
2. The situation creates thoughts as we begin to think about it and its potential outcomes—especially as they relate to us.

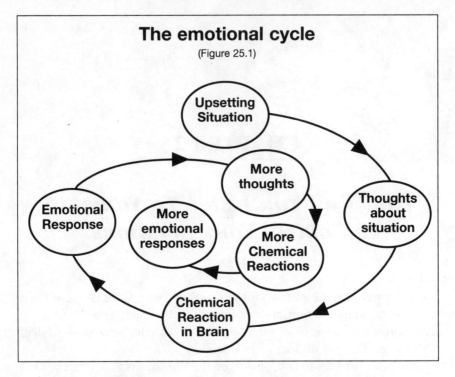

The emotional cycle
(Figure 25.1)

Upsetting Situation

More thoughts

Thoughts about situation

Emotional Response

More emotional responses

More Chemical Reactions

Chemical Reaction in Brain

3. Our thoughts create a chemical response in our brain.
4. It is this chemical response that creates our emotions—
   how we feel about the situation.
5. Our emotions create more thoughts about the situation,
   and as more thoughts are generated, more chemical
   responses, and more thoughts...

What is amazing about this situation and about how our bodies respond is that this whole process can take place in no more than a few seconds. Unless we are in control of our original reaction, our thoughts about the situation and our emotions take over and the real control that we should have had is taken away from us by an emotional overreaction.

As we have noted throughout this book, much of control comes down to awareness. When we are aware of how we, or our bodies, respond, we are in a much better position to control ourselves. Part of life is learning to control our emotions. This begins when we listen to ourselves. Begin to listen to the types of messages you send to others and to yourself. Listen.

One sign of an emotionally immature person is one who says,

"What you see is what you get." Another version of the same thing is, "That's just the way I am, you'll just have to put up with me." What others see is not what they need to get if we are able to gain control. "What you see is what you get," is fine for those who "go with the flow" of their emotions.

Emotions that are left unchecked can cause psychological damage, physical stress, and interpersonal problems. But checking our emotional reactions requires that we *do* something. Otherwise, we are left to our habitual reactions—the way we are. Too often, we feel, by not listening to our own messages, we give ourselves the wrong kind of self-talk. That is, when we listen to ourselves, what we hear ourselves saying are things like, "You make me so mad," or "That really bugs the hell out of me," or "Why is everyone out to get me upset?"

Often, we fight hard to tell ourselves that we are angry, hurt, upset, and unhappy. By listening to ourselves and becoming aware of our responses, we can tell ourselves that we are in control. We *can* take control of our reactions—the thoughts we have that trigger the chemical response that creates the emotions. The essential message is, "We are in control," although we can give ourselves this important message in a variety of ways:

- "I will not let my emotions control me."
- "I will not allow harmful emotions to get in my way."
- "I want to turn my feelings and emotions into forces of good."
- "I enjoy dealing with others in a calm, controlled manner."
- "I like who I am, and I am in control of my self."
- "I can be patient with and understanding of others."
- "I will do the things that remove harmful stress from my life."
- "I act in ways that bring calm contentment to my life and to the lives of those around me."
- "I have the habit of having positive emotions."
- "I find it easy to control my emotions."
- "I have good attitudes about myself and others."
- "I can be sensitive, warm, and open with others."
- "I express my feelings in a healthy, positive way."
- "I create strong, positive feelings and emotions."
- "I create the emotions that give me peace of mind, that improve my physical health, and that improve my relationships with others."

What occurs when we begin listening internally and use these positive statements is that we change the thoughts about situations—all situations. We begin giving ourselves controlled and specific positive perspectives. What we have done is to change the sieve or filter through which all perceptions come. When the nature of the filter is changed, our impressions of all situations are changed. With positive thoughts, there is less likelihood of chemical responses creating negative emotions and the cycle displayed in Figure 25.1 is stopped before it gets started.

Notice that to stop the cycle requires effort. We must *want* to change our behavior—our habits. Listening is a habit. How we listen to ourselves and the messages we give ourselves makes a difference in the way we control our emotions. We can start to take charge of our emotions if we just follow this simple prescription:

1. Become aware of how the emotional cycle occurs.
2. Realize the relationship between thoughts and emotions.
3. Listen to the negative messages we give ourselves.
4. Stop yourself when negative messages are being produced.
5. Change negative messages into positive ones by substituting some of the positive suggestions listed earlier.
6. Take charge of your life. It can make a major and important difference in the way you approach situations.
   Listen to yourself to control your emotions.

CHAPTER 26

How Can You Analyze Everyone's Goals?

When we begin discussing issues with people, we come to the table with a willingness to interact. There are situations where some individuals come to the table for appearance only, but those situations are extremes. In most cases, people come together with a desire to interact. A natural part of the interaction process is disagreement. This is a key point. This is like saying, "If you put two people together for any length of time, there will be conflict."

We all have different backgrounds, experiences, and personalities which were discussed in Chapters 6 and 7. We all filter and reduce information to fit our experiences and understandings. This is not necessarily bad. In every organization, it is important to have differing responses and to see things in a variety of ways. Without different perspectives, creativity and originality are lost. However, it is these same differences that bring on conflict.

THE WILLINGNESS TO INTERACT

Most people begin with a willingness to interact with the individuals they work with. Imagine yourself as a desk clerk in a hotel. You enter the hotel on that day with a willingness to interact with people. A customer walks in with a scowl on his face. He is in jeans and a ragged T-shirt. "Yo man, the room I was staying in last night had an air conditioner that..." At this point, you have initiated the downward cycle of listening in a conflict situation. That is, you have mentally cut off the speaker and allowed your filters to begin to control the interaction. The clothing, the scowl, and the language sent you messages that interfered with the message. Regardless of what he says about the room, you will defend the situation because your filters instinctively say that he is an inadequate judge of the situation. The downward cycle begins when we move from a willingness to interact to filters that speed our jump toward faulty conclusions.

THE OVERT STEP

In the downward cycle, your next response is probably going to be an overt or visible one. You may interrupt him verbally, or you may signal nonverbally that you are in disagreement with him, or that you disdain what he is saying. At this point, you are responding not to his perspective but, rather, to your own filters and reduction mechanisms. Consequently the conflict cycle will continue to regress, to sink, to continue its negative downward cycle.

THE COVERT STEP

After you have responded, the customer is still unhappy. He knows that you have not heard him. In fact, your response has worsened the situation, because he is now responding not to the problem, but to your response. As he begins to argue with you, your reaction is to mentally take the next step. It is a covert response. Rather than listening, you are preparing counter arguments to offset his tone, and you are thinking of how you can get rid of this troublemaker. Now you are mentally responding to his responses which are confirming your earlier filtered reaction.

THE CRITICAL POINT

You have reached the critical point in the conflict. It is here that either you will have an angry customer walk out on you, you will call security to throw him out, or he will demand your supervisor. As a result, there will either be third-party intervention, or something that dramatically changes the interaction. It is at this point that supervisors and mediators are called in to review a problem. It is a critical junction in the business world—you either keep a customer, and the five friends they tell, for life, or you lose them, and the ten other people they tell!

START BY STOPPING

If you are furious at this point, it will be a long upward battle to begin listening now. It is possible to do, but it takes incredible willpower. To listen now means admitting that you probably did not hear the person in the beginning—a difficult thing to do for even the humblest of people. But you do not want to lose a customer (or your next promotion) because you could not handle a situation. So you start by stopping the interaction.

It is here that you need to swallow hard and say, "I need to apologize. I don't think I listened carefully enough to understand the problem. Would you please start again, and explain the situation to make sure that I understand your concern?" Realize that at this point you are going back to the beginning—a willingness to hear the person. Can it be done? Yes, but only if you and the person have the time and the energy. Often, at this point, you and the other person are emotionally beyond the point of return. The only way is if you are willing to admit a breakdown in your own listening ability.

BACK TO H.E.A.R.

Asking to try again begins with a genuine willingness to *hear* the individual. You have to want to *hear* that individual, and demonstrate it. If you do not, quit now, or you will be wasting your time and his. Second, you have to *engage* that individual to demonstrate your willingness to listen. He is already upset. He already does not believe that you are hearing him. By engaging in paraphrasing and summarizing his main points, you are now taking the time to demonstrate your interest in getting the facts right. Also, you are helping to ensure that your own filters and reduction mechanisms are not blocking your understanding of the problem. If you are not getting what he is saying, and you summarize and paraphrase his main points incorrectly, he will quickly give you feedback.

When he is finished this time, *ask questions*. Preface your first question by saying, "I want to be certain that I understand the problem." By asking questions before responding, you demonstrate a desire to have all the facts and a willingness to be patient enough to study the situation and hear his side of the story. This is what earns you and your organization respect.

It is at this point where you *respond*. Remember that part of demonstrating that you have been listening comes in the response. It is here where you elect to disagree, if you wish to, in a fashion that explains why you disagree in terms of their perspective and from their facts. Or you can elect to agree and follow up on their concern.

How can you analyze everyone's goals?

1. Reveal a willingness to interact.
2. *H*ear the other person.
3. *E*ngage in paraphrasing and summarizing.
4. *A*sk questions.
5. *R*espond appropriately.

The best way we have to analyze others' goals is to make certain others have a complete (free and full) opportunity to express them. The best way we have to encourage free and full expression is to reveal a willingness to interact, and then put the H.E.A.R. method of listening into action.

CHAPTER 27

Why Doesn't Time Get You The Results You Want?

You have heard the clichés, "Time heals all wounds," or "If we can just wait long enough, the problem will solve itself," or "If we can just keep them talking, they will automatically solve the dispute." The idea is that time plays a significant part in decision making and problem solving. There is no doubt that it can; there is no doubt that it does. But time doesn't necessarily get you the results you want. Consider this example:

> The meeting was clearly filled with tension. The two supervisors told meeting participants about the ongoing problems with two warring factions in their respective departments. It had grown to the point where clearly a grievance from one of the two parties was going to be filed. It wasn't "if" it was going to be filed, it was just a question of "when" it would be filed. As the participants at the meeting discussed the problem, Tom mentioned the fact that the problem seemed to have escalated because of the failure of the two parties to listen to each other in the early stages of the dispute.
>
> It was at that point that the supervisor, Phyllis, stopped Tom. "Listen to me, and listen to me closely," she said directly to Tom in a frustrated voice, "We spent hours working with these two parties. In fact, I spent more time trying to help them listen to each other than in doing anything else. But the more I tried to get them to listen to each other, the more the conflict seemed to escalate and go public."

Often, it seems, we equate time with results. If we spend a lot of time on a subject, then we should get the results we want. Much of this thinking is programmed from our school days. The idea is that *if* we would give sufficient time to a course, we could get the "A" or "B" grade we desired. It was always a direct, causal link: time equaled the appropriate grade.

But the same idea does not necessarily carry over into conflict situations. The fact is, in high conflict situations, when listening skills are needed the most, studies demonstrate that people listen the least. More time does not mean more listening, better quality, excellent results, or even participant satisfaction!

Try something for us in the next conflict situation you face. Instead of spending excessive amounts of time trying to get the other person to listen to you, or even to get you to listen to the other person, start by having the other person—and yourself—listen to yourselves. It is a whole new way of approaching conflict situations.

People with poor listening skills often reflect poor self-appraisal skills. As a result, in conflict situations not only are they not hearing each other, they are not hearing themselves. Consequently they may not realize their own unreasonableness. Hurt people hurt others. When we strike out at the other person in conflict, we are probably better expressing our own hurt than we are trying to solve a problem, resolve a conflict, or hear what the other person is saying. If we can get in touch with that hurt, we are probably going to have a better base for understanding what the conflict is all about.

For example, in the earlier situation presented at the beginning of this chapter, rather than spending excessive amounts of time trying to get the two warring factions in their departments to listen to each other, Phyllis needed to change tactics. She needed to focus on helping each warring party listen to their demands, their own feelings (anger), and their own responses. Remember, in conflict situations when it comes to listening, times does not equal results. Time can magnify, distort, color, warp, misconstrue, alter, deform, misshape, bend, and twist.

I'm sure you have been in conflict situations that have not been resolved. You go away mad and angry. You go away so frustrated that the other side cannot see your strong, rational, and reasonable viewpoint. And what often happens as time passes, you also distort the other side's views. You make your side of the conflict even more perfect, more reasonable, and more satisfying to yourself. You are not the least bit concerned here with listening to yourself; you are simply

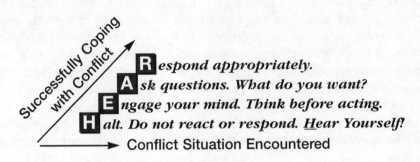

(Figure 27.1)

making yourself look better in your own eyes by distorting anything that disagrees with or conflicts with your side. Before conflicting parties can listen and understand others, they first have to listen and understand themselves.

So, how do you slow things down? How do you make it possible to listen to yourself when involved in a conflict situation? First, you are going to have to react differently than you ever have before. We have listed the appropriate response pattern in four steps:

Step 1: Stop! Before reacting or responding in any way, just stop. Do not react or respond in any way.

Step 2: Put your mind in gear before your mouth. Think about what you are about to say or do.

Step 3: Ask yourself right now: What do you want from this encounter? The answer to this question can give direction to or focus what is about to happen.

    a. What kinds of questions do you want answered?

    b. What solutions do you think will satisfy you? or the other person?

    c. What do you want from the other person?

    d. How is the other person likely to respond or react to your action or comments?

Step 4: Now, and only now, after thought (and a short time) has occurred, an appropriate, thoughtful, sensitive response should take place.

In this way, you are using time in a different way. You are structuring time positively—so that it can work to your benefit. Phyllis could stop the warring parties by using these steps. What would be better for her would be to separate the parties, rather than having them try to listen to each other. Then, she could go through the above steps with each one—separated from the other. In this way, both parties would have a much clearer idea of what *they* wanted before trying to understand what the other party wanted.

In Figure 27.1, we show how the above four steps could be placed into a convenient, memorable intervention strategy—one with which we have become familiar, but with a slightly different twist.

CHAPTER 28

How Can You Become A Peacemaker?

Helga was angry. She had to work in Food Service for the week, and she had learned that Jodie had just been transferred from Food Service. Like many of the seasonal employees, working the kitchen during the summer was not something Helga preferred. She simply endured it knowing that the others had to contend with the same problems she did. Now it seemed that Jodie was getting special treatment. Helga knew that Jodie was scheduled to work Food Service because the head cook, Dennis, had told her so. But she had also overheard the executive director and boss, Ed, overrule Dennis and change Jodie's work schedule. Helga was now frustrated and mad because she thought an injustice had occurred.

Helga knew that Jodie did not want to work in Food Service. She had overheard Jodie tell another employee in the staff lounge that "there was no way" she would work in Food Service the coming week. And, what's more, she had seen Ed, the executive director, talking to Tom, the employee who was later assigned to the Food Service program replacing Jodie. Helga knew how to put two and two together.

For Helga, this was obviously not fair. Tom was forced into the Food Service department while someone else got special privileges. So Helga, frustrated and angry, told Tonya—the girl Tom was dating. She told Tonya that Tom was put into the new position because Jodie had gone to the boss, Ed, and threatened to quit if she wasn't transferred.

This information made Tonya furious. Tonya reasoned, "Why should Tom suffer because Jodie didn't want to do her job?" So she went to Tom and told him Jodie was getting special favors from the boss, and that is why he ended up being transferred into Food Service. This upset Tom, who told the other kitchen workers. They, too, became angry. This all happened within an eight-hour shift.

The next day on lunch break, Tonya and Tom told Nancy, who was working in Jodie's new department, that Jodie was getting special favors in order to get out of pulling her share of the workload. Nancy, in turn, told the other workers in Jodie's new department that Jodie could choose her work assignments because she was getting special favors from Ed, the boss. As a result, the other members of Jodie's new department began to ostracize and shun her.

The supervisor of Jodie's new department, Brenda, began to notice conflicts between Jodie and the other members of the staff—particularly Nancy. In fact, the animosity at times seemed vicious. Being unsure of what to do, Brenda went to the boss, Ed, wondering how she could manage the personality conflicts in her department, now that Jodie had been added to her work team.

The same day, the issue surfaced during a managerial staff meeting. The Food Service supervisor, Leroy, observed that his staff did not seem to like Jodie. Now, Brenda was reporting that her staff did not like her very well either. The managers looked to the boss, Ed, for what to do.

Does this situation sound far-fetched? Could it happen? Before answering, read on. There are a few more pieces to add to the puzzle. What Helga did not know was that Jodie was *not* avoiding work or even a specific assignment to Food Service. Jodie was willing to work Food Service, but she was transferred because of a private family problem that required her being able to take time off without disrupting the flow of the department. In Food Service there are continuous, unavoidable deadlines that must be complied with. For one person to leave that department breaks the flow. So when Helga overheard the transfer, she only got *part* of the information, but she reacted to the information she received accordingly—without knowing the full story.

And there is another piece of the puzzle missing too. What Helga and Tonya did not know was that Tom was not transferred unwillingly. When given the choice between his current assignment and Food Service, he agreed to the transfer. He neglected to mention this to Helga and Tonya after they told him why Jodie was transferred. After hearing their story, his move didn't look quite as good, so he chose not to tell them the transfer was his choice.

What Nancy, Tonya, and Tom did not know was that Helga wanted to be transferred to the department that Jodie was transferred to, but she lacked qualifications. When Jodie received the transfer and she didn't, it only reinforced her own frustration and insecurity. This made it easy for her to go to Tonya to try to stir up trouble for Jodie.

Of course, Ed, the boss, and his departmental managers, Leroy and Brenda, did not know any of this during the departmental staff meeting. They were surmising that it was just a personality conflict—that it was Jodie's problem alone, since she had had problems in two different departments.

Does this kind of thing happen? You'd better believe it. Not only does it happen, it happens every day of every year. Maybe it doesn't occur with the complexity of this instance, but this type of conflict occurs on a continuing basis. This particular situation not only occurs, we experienced it as it unfolded.

An important point to remember is that conflict is inevitable. The real question is "How can listening help managers deal with conflicts?" Most organizational conflict does not center around personalities; it centers around information and communication. If you want to be a peacemaker, you start by listening, not by trying to solve a personality problem. When conflicts can be framed as communication problems, they can be solved as communication problems.

What usually happens is that we diagnose problems to be personality conflicts between workers—just as Ed, Leroy, and Brenda diagnosed Jodie's problem. In the above situation, who was having the personality conflict? On the surface, the boss and the supervisors saw the conflict as Nancy and Jodie being unable to get along, or between Jodie and her co-workers in two separate departments. So, to deal with the conflict, both Leroy and Brenda did what most people do— they tried to get Jodie and Nancy to change—or, at the minimum, to get Jodie! But change was virtually impossible because in the background were Helga, Tonya, and Tom (and the other department personnel) feeding the problem.

So, how do you listen in the midst of conflict? You start by changing the question. Not, how do you listen? But, to whom do you listen? Listening in situations where tensions run high begins with asking questions of people who are *not* involved. Most of the time, they will have an idea of what is going on. Interestingly enough, the office grapevine in these situations is a valuable resource.

A researcher studying the office grapevine found an amazing fact: the office grapevine almost always is partially true! Most of the time it is not the whole story. The thing to remember is that when people receive information on the grapevine, they perceive it to be true! They react first as if they have the full story (and they fill in the details of what they did not get), and, second, they believe what they hear.

When managers talk to those not involved, they need to keep a low profile. They need to listen and ask questions rather than give opinions. They need to think of themselves as trying to put together an intricate puzzle. Every person with whom they speak holds a piece of the puzzle. The important thing to keep in mind is that there are multiple realities in every situation and these multiple realities depend on perception. While each person sees the situation differently, no one may be lying. They are simply not seeing the situation with all the information. Theirs is simply one way of seeing things.

The only way that you can begin to understand a conflict is by getting all, or at least most of, the pieces of the puzzle. To take this puzzle analogy one step further, don't finish the puzzle by giving away pieces. Ask questions, but refrain from the urge to set people straight or to help them frame their reality. Since you don't have all the pieces to the puzzle either, and you may not see the whole puzzle, you need to act like the picture is incomplete. In all instances, you are trying to get others to open up and to share their piece or pieces of the puzzle.

After you have some picture of what is happening, then it is time to listen to the parties involved in the conflict. You can begin the peace process by listening to the parties individually first, as indicated in the last chapter. This is *not* the time to talk to *both* parties—especially at the same time. As a matter-of-fact, it is not time to talk to either party! It is time to *listen* to each party—separately—one at a time.

Also, this is not the time to bring all parties into one room and get the conflict out in the open, although this is a natural tendency. "Let's get this thing out in the open so we can solve it!" You can just hear this being said. Incidentally, if you *do* yield to the temptation of getting both parties into one room, you may find that both parties have found one common enemy—*YOU!*

Rarely are conflicts solved in group meetings. This is mainly because everyone wants to talk. Everyone wants to give his or her version of what happened, what the conflict is, their view of the situation, or their proposed solution. When everyone wants to talk, and only a few get to talk, everyone leaves the meeting unhappy. The real art of solving conflicts begins one-on-one in back rooms where people can listen with good listening ears and put the full H.E.A.R. process to work. (See Chapter 15.)

When you, as a manager, listen to the parties individually, allow them to go through the process outlined in the last chapter. After listening to themselves, they need to be given a chance to describe the conflict. Many times the problem is one of two things: 1) inadequate information, or 2) poor communication and, thus, a misunderstanding between the parties. If it can be described as a communication problem it can be solved as a communication problem.

If, after listening to both parties and other uninvolved employees, you realize that the conflict is between these two parties, then you can take action with the two of them. But if, like the situation first introduced in this chapter, the conflict has spread more widely, then you don't need to waste your time bringing the two parties together—at least initially—you need to work at distributing information widely.

If the intent is to distribute information widely, this process can be started by making sure that both parties individually have the same amount of information. In the situation described at the beginning of this chapter, no one had all the information. Everyone involved reacted based on the information they had.

To begin to deal with this kind of conflict situation, begin by giving the participants a broader perspective. Remember, that you did not have a broader perspective until you listened. So, to ensure that the parties involved have a broader perspective, you need to make certain *they* are listening. This is best done by meeting them one on one, then giving them all the information concerning the conflict situation. This is not the time to blame, criticize, censure, condemn, denounce, reprehend, or accuse. Rather, this is the time to let each participant realize that he or she did not have all the information and that part of every conflict is misunderstanding.

Also, this is the time to introduce the broader information to those with whom you talked earlier, the uninvolved people from whom you received important pieces of the puzzle. These people are probably wondering what is going on. The key is not to focus on who did or said what, but to give them the broader picture of what the problem is and how it will be resolved. Be careful! If you give too much information you risk having the direct participants—those actually involved in the conflict—lose face. You need to protect the participants by ensuring that no participant is humiliated in the process.

When meeting with any of the involved and uninvolved parties, it is important to frame the conflict as a communication problem.

Framing it as a "personality problem" encourages people to take the position "that's just the way we are." This implies that change is not an option. To frame a conflict as a communication problem implies that with information and better communication, the conflict can be solved. When giving out the broader information, the importance of listening as a tool for improved relationships also can be mentioned.

This is the time to lay the proper groundwork for workers to listen to each other. For example, they can be told that listening is more than just hearing. They can be introduced to the H.E.A.R. method, and they can be told exactly how to put this method into practice.

If the conflict was just between the two participants, then now is the time to get the two of them together. This will not be an easy meeting. But, it will be better if you have reinforced two things before the meeting. First, the participants do not have to like each other, but they do have to listen and speak with each other in a civil fashion. Second, and probably the biggest reason why people lose their jobs, they must try to get along with each other. While we don't have research documenting this, our hunch is that the biggest reason why people lose their jobs is not incompetence—inability to do the job they are supposed to do—but the inability to get along with others.

In this meeting, the H.E.A.R. method is probably the best tool to use to help the participants listen to each other. A quick review of Chapter 15 will help you recall the complete method. We have summarized it under point seven below. Have one party speak for five minutes while the other party practices the H.E.A.R. method. Make sure both parties *H*ear the other. Have the listening party *E*ngage the speaker by summarizing what has been said. This is particularly important. This will ensure that each party is getting the meaning of the message. Have them *A*sk questions. Have them offer the appropriate *R*esponse. Then reverse the process. This will be time consuming, but it allows each party to hear and understand each side.

Again, you want to push for solutions that encourage and improve the communication process. Each party involved can and should be asked to come up with ideas to improve communication. Notice, the point is not to change the other person. The point is not to revolutionize their relationship. The point is not to solve the problem. The point is simply to offer ideas that will improve their ability to listen and to understand what the other person is saying on a day-to-day basis. This is the first step towards reducing the conflict in any relationship, in any workplace, in any family, or in any place where people have to work with one another.

How, then, do you listen in the midst of conflict? Here, we offer a brief review of the main points of this chapter:

1. Stop! Do not react or respond.
2. Listen.
   a. What information can you discover?
   b. To whom do you need to listen?
3. Investigate the office grapevine.
4. Ask questions.
   a. Refrain from giving opinions.
   b. Keep a low profile.
5. Listen now to the parties involved in the conflict.
   a. Listen to them separately.
   b. Listen to their whole story.
   c. Let them describe the conflict.
6. Try to frame the conflict as a communication problem. (Remember, if it is described as a communication problem, then it can be resolved as a communication problem, and the personalities of the people involved are not at issue.)
7. Encourage participants to use the H.E.A.R. method:
   *H*ear the message. Prepare yourself so that you can physically hear all that is being said.
   *E*ngage in summarizing what you heard the individual saying.
   *A*sk questions about what you heard. Don't forget to listen so they can give answers to your questions.
   *R*eact appropriately. Either tell them what you think of what they said, or tell them when you will get back to them about what you think of what they said.

PART EIGHT

How Can Managers Listen In Meetings?

CHAPTER 29

What Are Your Barriers To Listening In Meetings?

I'm sure you have heard all the cute stories and disparaging remarks about meetings and committees: "God so loved the world, that he did not send a committee"..."if Columbus were a committee, he'd still be in search of America"..."a conference is a gathering of important people who singly can do nothing, but together can decide that nothing can be done"..."a meeting is a thing that takes a week to do what one good person can do in an hour"... "a camel is just a horse put together by a committee." Referring to the number of people involved in making decisions, it also has been said that meetings are like having "too many cooks in the kitchen," or "too many fingers in the pie."

When a group of managers was asked to rate the times that listening was most problematic or difficult, they rated listening during meetings as being the biggest problem (Hunt and Cusella, 1983). Part of the reason for this is that in meetings we contribute the least, but have to listen the most. And, no matter how fast someone talks, we can still think about twice as fast. As a result, the temptation is to allow your mind to wander.

When we sit in meetings, the first thing that begins running through our mind when someone begins to speak is, "What is your point?" We are driven by the desire to have this question answered, and when people do not get to the point, besides being annoyed, the main temptation is to think beyond them. The problem with this is that often people make their point in strange and obtuse ways. They find a hundred different ways to skirt the issue before finally hitting their point—if they ever hit it at all! As a result, our minds wander in another direction, and often we have missed the central idea of their contribution.

The bottom line is that most of us are selfish. We are driven by our own needs, wants, and desires. Consequently when someone is speaking and mentally we ask the question, "What's the point?," we are not asking what is the point, we are really asking, "How does this relate to me?" If we do not see the answer easily, we become lazy! We begin to assume that if it does not relate to us, then we have no reason to listen. We rationalize that the subject is taking time that could better be used for more important thoughts and that we have no need to know this information. The No. 1 barrier to listening effectively in meetings is not poor presenters; it is our own lack of self-discipline. The first barrier to listening effectively in meetings is failure to discipline ourselves to listen well.

We knew of an employee who thought he had an answer to every problem. Someone in the staff meeting would begin to present a problem situation, and before the presenter had finished, this individual was already giving the solution. You see, his mind was made up before the presenter even began. In fact, his opinions were formed, and they were like Henry Ford selling the Model T: "You can have it in any color you want as long as it's black." You could get this fellow's opinion on any subject. Regardless of what you said, the information you gave, or the opinions you supplied, his opinion did not change. Was he listening to the issues? Of course not. He was too busy forming solutions and deciding how to phrase his previously formed opinion. Was he well liked? No. Did he last long on the job? No. He was his own worst enemy.

His opinions and narrow perspectives gave him no reason to listen. While he could not see it himself, those around him felt that he actually believed that he did not need other views. When you are tempted to close your mind because you don't like or don't agree with another opinion, or you think you have all the answers, you have created a barrier to listening. You have become your own worst enemy!

Because we are bored or distracted in meetings, we do not signal to others that we are listening. Remember Herbert who was a terrible participant at meetings? Herb always looked like he was half asleep. He slouched in his chair. He held his head up with his arms. He said little or nothing. Sometimes Herb would even nod off. He always looked like his mind was thousands of miles away. The second barrier to listening in meetings is not providing presenters, speakers, or contributors with any feedback that we are listening. To get more information and to get better information, feedback is necessary.

When people are speaking who we don't like or respect, it is easy to ignore them. The temptation is to avoid giving them active signals that we are listening—because we are not! The temptation is to concentrate on what we don't like about them rather than the content of what they are saying. When we are tempted to respond to others for who they are or for what they look like, rather than for what they are saying, then we are experiencing a listening barrier. It happens often. The cliché, "You cannot tell a book by its cover," offers an opposing view; but we often attempt to tell books (people) by their covers (appearances). We do this because it is easy to do and second, we are lazy. Third, we are victims of our stereotypes and predispositions. And, fourth, often we get reinforcement for doing so because sometimes we are proven correct. So the third barrier to listening in meetings is our failure to concentrate on the content of what is being said—being distracted by looks, assumptions, or manner of dress.

That is why the following three listening barriers are probably the most difficult to overcome during meetings:

1. Failure to discipline ourselves to listen.
2. Failure to provide active signals that we are listening.
3. Failure to concentrate on the content of the message.

Everyone experiences them. No one likes unproductive meetings. But it is important to remember that productivity in meetings begins with communication. And communication is a two-way street. Speakers may be unproductive in the way they present information, but your listening barriers may be dragging you down to their level of poor productivity.

How can we *not* let listening barriers prevent us from effective communication in meetings?:

1. Go to meetings with a purpose or goal. Think: there is something in this for me.
2. Convince yourself to listen only for ideas. Avoid distractions from this goal. Do not be distracted by appearances, attitudes, emotions, or extraneous factors. Stay focused. Tell yourself: "I will listen only for ideas." Use positive self-talk to focus your concentration and your thinking.

3. Script yourself for productivity. If you enter the meeting being dependent on the other participants, then your communication level is only as effective as they are. Create your own, independent script by setting your own agenda. Don't allow others' productivity levels to control yours.

Create an active agenda to:

1. learn
2. understand
3. ask questions
4. gain quality information.

These concepts will stimulate your listening ability.

CHAPTER 30

How Can You Use Listening To Build Teamwork In Meetings?

Cohesiveness occurs when we identify with a group or organization. This could be a family, a business we work for, an organization, a political party, or a club. In a sense, cohesion occurs within a group when everyone is united behind the group's mission or purpose. This is not to say there is no conflict within the group. In fact, it may be just the opposite.

Often, groups and organizations that avoid conflict are not very cohesive. Why? Because in their efforts to avoid conflict, often they do not deal with issues that are inherent in the group process. These issues might involve, for example, how decisions are made, how tasks are delegated, how roles are assigned, or how members are recruited. As a result, sometimes groups will all too hastily follow a faulty path of reasoning, make a poor decision, or take an inappropriate action just to avoid conflict.

We remember one group in which a whole set of rules were established just because one member of the group desired specific courses of action to follow in all meetings. When the member left the group, the group realized that it was the rules that were inhibiting the group and prohibiting progress, growth, and creativity. Everything, it seemed, had to be "by the rules." They rescinded them all. Their informal structure was sufficient. They had set up a wealth of unnecessary rules and spent a tremendous amount of time and effort just to avoid conflict with one group member who, it turned out, went on to create similar problems in the next group he joined.

In cohesive groups, there is a strong identification with the group.

Members feel more comfortable with each other, and there is a strong sense of cooperation and mutual support. In the group just referred to above, the member for whom all the rules were created felt insecure, unconfident, uncertain, and unsure. When people do not feel comfortable with one another, they tend to be reserved. They hesitate to take risks. They are reluctant to share new ideas. They are afraid of being shot down by the group. All of these were evident in the group above.

Cohesion within groups encourages people to share new ideas and concepts. It gives people the freedom to be creative without being afraid of getting shot down. The group referred to above felt shackled by the rules they felt forced to create. Prior to rule setting, the group had operated informally and comfortably. The rules broke their solidarity and togetherness.

Several years ago we conducted a workshop in group communication. We broke the workshop into two groups. For twelve weeks we had each group work independently at designing a unique business idea. As we observed the two groups, we noticed the first group was respectful and reserved. Their discussion was polite and soft-spoken. They were quiet in the room before and after the sessions. Ideas in this group were given hesitantly.

The second group was a zoo. They started out quietly, but by the fourth week, we almost had to shout to get their attention. They were talking and laughing loudly with each other before and after sessions. During their group discussions, they were respectful, but not orderly. They laughed at their own mistakes while encouraging people to share their thoughts.

The second group was more creative, more willing to work, and more concerned about producing a better product. Not only were they willing to work because of a material reward, they worked hard because they enjoyed each other and identified with the nature of the group. They produced a superior product.

The first group was punishing. While they were polite in sessions, after a session we observed them talking in groups of two and three about other members of the group. When mistakes were made or things did not seem to go well within the group, rather than bring it up to the entire group, they brought it up to each other after a meeting. They began to scapegoat each other, and eventually the group became fragmented and frustrated. They lacked cohesion. And what was interesting as well, they were unhappy with their final product.

Cohesiveness allows members to feel comfortable with each other and the task at hand. It takes time, energy, and effort. Effective managers will seek to build cohesion (or member identification with the group) and to improve meetings and productivity. But, realize, too, that cohesion often means managers will find themselves feeling uncomfortable because the joke of the day may be about them, or at their expense. Groups may seem disrespectful at times. It will probably feel as if members value the group more than the manager. But cohesion begins with the manager, and it makes a manager more effective in the long run.

Building cohesion begins with listening. Smart managers learn that each member comes to group meetings with differing needs and desires. One person in a meeting may be interested in making a good impression with the boss. Another person may be careful to not offend anybody. Someone else may want to get the meeting over with and get back to "real" work. Another person may want to control the meeting entirely. The point is that in every meeting different people bring different goals. Cohesion occurs when managers are able to give each member enough ownership in the meeting so that he or she feels as if his or her needs are being met. Ownership is what brings group identification and cohesion to meetings. It begins when managers listen to the people within meetings: what are *their* wants, needs, and desires?

Since we tend to approach situations from a speaking perspective rather than from a listening perspective, managers are tempted to begin meetings by speaking rather than listening. They might, for example, cover some ideas discussed in the last meeting. They might go over some announcements. Or, they might give an agenda to the group. Agendas are great; we hate to go to meetings where an agenda is not followed. But agendas can become managers' ways for controlling groups.

The first thing managers can do is change their format. If the group is relatively small (from three members to fifteen), managers could start the meeting differently. They could ask members if they have agenda items that will need to be discussed. In this way, members are given their first identification with the group. In this way, members are allowed to identify reasons why *they* are present. In this way, members are allowed to speak first, and managers have a chance to listen.

Second, managers can listen more sensitively. They need to listen in meetings for problems, struggles, failures, or successes that are common among members. As a manager, you are more likely to know what is going on with all of the employees. Often, employees do not have this big picture. Consequently, employees often feel isolated. They feel like they are just one small, insignificant cog in a huge machine. After listening for common elements, managers need to highlight these common areas when they speak. By doing this, they help members identify with each other.

Often, employees feel they work alone on significant problems. They begin to believe that only they experience failure. They may feel they are the only ones feeling frustrated or anxious. When managers are able to identify areas of common experience, group members begin to understand the importance of sharing ideas or problems simply because someone else may also have experienced the same problem. This ability to *discover commonness* demonstrates that failure is not terminal. It is the way it is handled that kills.

The third thing managers can do to build cohesion is to engage in *team building and empowerment.* For example, managers can get group members to brainstorm for solutions. Managers should hesitate to speak when employees are brainstorming ideas to solve problems. This forces groups to develop strategies for problem solving rather than simply relying on managers to solve them. This, in turn, develops group ownership in both meetings and in the solutions that are generated. Groups begin to develop their own culture rather than waiting for managers to set the tone for what is acceptable. The manager builds the team then reaps the benefits and products of the team by listening and responding to the team efforts. The manager reaps the benefits and the employees are empowered! Of course, this is a tough thing to do.

As managers, we come to believe that it is our job to solve problems. Our employees also may believe that it is our job to solve problems. And, many managers believe the way to solve problems is by taking the bull by the horns and tell people how to deal with situations. This is a no-win trap! Even if we are correct, we lose. The more successful we are at solving the problems, the more likely it is that employees will look to us in meetings to give solutions. When we fail to solve problems, it is our responsibility and not the employees who may have created the problem. As tempting as it is to play "God," don't do it.

A manager's job is not to solve problems. As managers your job is to *facilitate* employee effectiveness. This is employee empowerment. This means helping employees develop strategies to solve problems. And, this means learning to listen in meetings. Think of it this way. It is rare that power does not change how or what is said. If a manager speaks too soon, group members will gravitate to what they think that manager wants to hear, rather than saying what may be the best idea. This stifles creativity. By listening, summarizing, and hesitating to speak in meetings, managers allow groups to build cohesion through solving problems creatively. This is empowerment!

The concept of not solving problems has two benefits. First, the combination of ideas that group members generate is probably superior. It has been proven that two heads, in general, are better than one! By speaking too soon, managers not only may lose the team spirit, but, potentially, they may lose the opportunity for success. Second, when managers are on vacation, sick, traveling, out of town, or unable to attend meetings, employees are still able to be creative and productive. They have been previously empowered to be effective. They have built a pattern for problem solving, and also they have a group identity already in place—secure and supportive. Should a crisis or problem occur, employees can still function effectively; they have been empowered by an effective manager.

It may be a boost to our ego when we come back from an absence and everybody wants to see us about solving all kinds of problems, but it is not the sign of an effective manager. The most effective managers are those who can leave and not worry about coming back to a work force that is ineffective, tied up, confused, and unproductive because of a lack of problem-solving skills, employee infighting, and finger pointing. Remember that it may not be because of a *lack* of skills, it can also be because they do not perceive that problem solving is within their jurisdiction! If they don't think they should be doing it, they won't!

Effective managers listen enough in meetings to know that their employees are capable. They listen long enough so that their employees are able to witness their own capabilities. They listen long enough to empower their employees to not only generate solutions, but to take action on those solutions that are agreed on. In this way, employees are encouraged to tap their own potential and capitalize on their own creativity. It is creative management, and effective management, and it works because it is dependent on effective listening!

Managers can build teamwork in meetings by (1) changing the format, (2) listening more sensitively, and (3) team building and empowerment. Empower by listening effectively and letting employees solve problems.

CHAPTER 31

What Three Listening "Rights" Do You Need To Develop A Productive Discussion?

Let's go back to one of the basic and fundamental reasons for the existence of this book: the fallacy that listening is a passive process. This translates into the philosophy, or idea, that in meetings, you simply have to sit back, relax, and soak it all up. In this chapter we advocate not only that you be an active listener, as we discussed in Chapter 14, but that you become an aggressive listener as well.

To develop a climate for a full and productive discussion, you need to demand certain listening "rights." If you do not, you will fall back on what is familiar—speaking. To use these listening "rights" you have to do something. That is, it is an active process. We will discuss the three most basic listening "rights."

The first "right" you have as an aggressive listener in a meeting is your "right" to cut off interrupters and demand that people have the opportunity to finish their thought. When did we start giving the floor to people in meetings simply because they are aggressive speakers? It is time to stop allowing individuals who cannot control their mouths to dominate meetings!

Corporate America must learn that letting people talk does not suggest knowledge, nor does it equate with leadership, represent good ideas,or reveal wisdom! In fact, if we want to create an atmosphere where discussion is productive, it is time that we aggressively pursue the right to listen to everyone in the meeting.

Sometimes the people who speak the least have the best ideas.

The problem is that often these people do not get a chance to share these ideas. Often people are shoved aside by the more aggressive or more articulate talkers. We once knew a colleague, Diane, who was extremely quiet in meetings. She rarely spoke, and when she did, her more aggressive colleagues often interrupted her. And yet, after the meetings, when we asked her what she thought of the decisions reached at these meetings, she had the most insightful perspective. She had intelligent ideas that should have been heard and used in the meetings.

Privately we asked Diane point blank, "Why don't you share your ideas in the meetings?" We told her not only was she hurting her promotional opportunities, but also she had significant thoughts that deserved attention. Her response was interesting and valuable. "Why fight it? I'm not taken seriously, and it's not worth it to be the bitch." It might not have been worth it to her, but the senior executives, Dan and Lou, knew that her ideas were valuable to them! What they did was to change the situation in such a way that her ideas could be heard. They opened channels and protected her right to share.

As researchers, we studied listening in small groups. At one point—and more out of curiosity than anything else—we asked members of these small groups why some people spoke more and some people spoke less in the meetings. The members of the groups who were talkative thought the quiet members did not have anything to say. The quiet members, on the other hand, said they did not have a chance to speak. The point is this: most everyone has something to say, but unless we aggressively demand listening, many of our most intelligent people will not be heard.

When aggressive talkers think "speak," not "listen," they move aggressively in meetings. They do not pause, they do not hesitate, and they do not respect the "rights" and needs of their less-aggressive meeting members. Why? Because they do not like dead air. And they quickly fill dead air, whether this means treading on the rights of others or not. It is not thoughtless behavior as much as it is expedient and efficient. But to nontalkers it looks thoughtless!

In the businesses where we have worked there is something called survival of the fittest. Being the best means getting and using the best ideas from employees. It starts with the *first* right: the right to aggressively listen by demanding that people stop interrupting and start listening.

We learned a valuable lesson in the organizations where we have worked. Employees should never have to be viewed as bitches just to be heard. And managers, supervisors, bosses, and directors have a responsibility—an obligation—to make certain that such situations never occur!

Second, you have the right to ignore someone who seeks to distract you during the course of a meeting. We can remember sitting in a meeting and having a good friend, Todd, lean over and whisper a message to us. The message was amusing, but it had nothing to do with what was going on in the meeting. As the meeting progressed, Todd tried to do this on a regular basis. The first time this happened, we politely responded by leaning towards him and listening to what he had to say.

But the second time, the third time, and the fourth time, we ignored Todd's nonverbal signals that he wanted to whisper a message to us. After the meetings he indicated that he was offended that we had ignored him. If he was offended, he certainly should have been! We know this sounds harsh, but the bottom line is that if you want to listen effectively, if you want a climate for open discussion, if you want to encourage others to express their ideas in full, free, productive discussion, then you must stay with the mainstream of the meeting regardless of how boring, uninteresting, or dull it has become.

Let's not sugar coat it. Whispering to people during a meeting is both rude and distracting! Of course, there *are* times when it is necessary. But there are far too many meetings where side conversations prevent effective listening and, consequently, damage the listening climate. You have the right to aggressively ignore people who try to repeatedly whisper messages to you. We are not going to discuss what happens when managers practice the habit of whispering messages to people during presentations. Suffice it to say that what goes around, comes around.

Third, you have the right to ask for clarification. Language is a tricky medium. The English language has countless words with multiple ways of being interpreted. Consequently misunderstanding is not only possible, it is a natural part of the communication process. Since each individual will take what he or she hears and bring meaning to it based upon his or her context of knowledge, multiple interpretations are natural and expected occurrences. Meeting success occurs when people leave meetings holding a similar (at least closely similar) understanding about what has been discussed and decided.

We have all been in meetings where a decision had been made and everyone left thinking they understood what was supposed to happen next. Two weeks later, at the next staff meeting, the boss asked the results of the action. Half the people look at John, while the rest look at Cindy. What happened? People framed the information according to their context and no one was listening aggressively enough to hear the contextual framing and ask for clarification. What happened? Nothing happened! That's the point!

The aggressive listener creates a meeting environment where asking for clarification is not only non-offensive, but expected. Productivity occurs when people use clarification as a tool to listen successfully.

So, once again, what are the three rights to making meetings effective?

(1) You have the right to demand that everyone gets a chance to speak and to finish their thought without interruption.

(2) You have the right to ignore people who are distracting you by whispering or passing notes to you.

(3) You have the right to ask for clarification.

CHAPTER 32

How Can You Use Internal Synergy In One-on-One Meetings?

The word "synergy" means to work together, a combined or cooperative force or action. The concept of synergism boils down to two people getting more done working together than they would separately. There is a story of Irving Berlin waiting on tables in Chinatown. While serving customers, he thought up the first line for a new song. He went to his musical neighbor, Nick, and asked him to help. Together, Irving and Nick wrote the words and music to *My Sweet Marie from Sunny Italy.* This song was the hit that started Irving Berlin on his career, a career that began because of synergism.

Most people work better creatively when teamed up with the right partner. Collaboration induces effort, spurs our powers of association, and often causes results to occur. But what most people do not realize, is that it does not necessarily require a second physical person to get positive synergistic results.

The point of synergism is that you stimulate and motivate each other when you work together. This increases your productivity in ways that are unlikely to occur when you work separately on the same project. It was Thomas Carlyle who wrote, "The lightning spark of thought, generated in the solitary mind, awakens its likeness in another mind." The question here is, how does this work internally when you are listening to someone else in a one-on-one meeting?

It begins with a concept developed by a man named George Herbert Mead. Through extensive research, Mead found that when a person does something or behaves in a certain way, there are actually two parts working internally. The first is the "I," the "I" that is the part of you that takes action. It is this part of you that maintains eye contact, nods to recognize something that has been said, or asks a question. The second part is the "me." The "me" justifies or condemns; it evaluates the actions the "I" takes.

If you begin to interrupt someone instead of listening, the "me" either says "Yes, he (or she) is on the wrong track" and this justifies your interruption. Or the "me" internally says "Whoa, you are beginning to talk without letting the other person finish." Either way, the two work together to push you to be a better listener, or they work separately—with the "I" behaving and the "me" evaluating—based on the desires of the "I."

Remember, since communication is a form of behavior, every time you communicate, a part of you (the "me") stands back and judges your behavior. So, while the "I" is listening, the "me" is evaluating the responses (i.e., the behaviors and attitudes) that the "I" is acting on. You are internally making evaluative decisions at the same time you are externally behaving. Here are some evaluative decisions:

1. Should I interrupt?
2. Is this person making sense?
3. How does this relate to me?
4. Should I correct this misinformation or let it go?
5. Does he or she know how to talk correctly?
6. Does this person know how to dress properly?
7. Why is this person getting so emotional?
8. Why is this person going on and on without end?
9. How does this person know this information?
10. Does this person or this information merit my close attention?

You can probably think of many, many other "internalized evaluative decisions" you make while others are talking. This decision-making or evaluative process becomes interruptive if it directs our attention internally to our own attitudes and behaviors—as any of the above questions would.

The evaluative process is distracting, too, if it calls attention to behaviors that do not externally focus on understanding what is being said—the content. Certainly questions 4, 5, and 6 do this. They internally guide attention away from the content of what is being said to other items such as correct speech, dress, and emotions.

For synergistic behavior to occur, for us to get the most out of conversations, for us to remain focused on the content of what is being said, we have to realize that both the actor and the evaluator (the "I" and the "me") within us, have to work together so that our listening behavior capitalizes on what is being said both verbally and nonverbally. Internal synergism occurs when the "I" and the "me"—the actor and the evaluator—work together within us.

You can begin doing this by going into meetings focused on what your *outcome* goal is for that meeting. Is this an employee evaluation? If so, your outcome goal is going to be different than if an employee is coming to talk to you about a personal problem. You need to think about this before the meeting! Thinking about your outcome goal allows the "I" to develop behaviors that are appropriate for that outcome. For example, if it is a personal problem, empathic listening coupled with reflective questions are appropriate behaviors.

What if the meeting has to do with a new product or a new line of products? The outcome or goal is different from an employee evaluation meeting. The outcome goal may be trying to understand the new product, how it relates to other company products, and the various new markets this product or line of products is designed to tap. The outcome goal clearly would be obtaining information. The "I" behaviors appropriate for that outcome goal might be active listening coupled with information-acquisition questions. And since this is likely to be a common type of meeting, many of the questions could be planned in advance.

When you go into a meeting with outcome goals in mind, this directs the evaluative side—the "me"—to call the "I" into accountability when you are tempted to stray from the listening behaviors that help you reach your outcome goals. In this way, the two can work together to reinforce and encourage proper behaviors.

In the beginning, for the greatest amount of internal synergy to take place, you need to briefly write down the outcome goals and meeting behaviors that will help you reach your goals before the meeting. Having it on paper reinforces both the right behaviors and your internal evaluative processes during the meeting. In this way, you have thought through the process, which means you will have some control over habitual or gut-level responses—the same old behaviors you engaged in before.

As you write down the outcome goals and meeting behaviors, try to provide yourself with a visual picture of you actually performing these behaviors. Visualization works in a cybernetic or corrective manner. Think, for example, of your furnace thermostat at home.

When the temperature gets too cold, the furnace kicks in because the thermostat measuring the temperature acts correctively to adjust the furnace behaviors according to the desired outcome—the previously set house temperature. When you visualize your goals for a meeting, and the types of behaviors needed to accomplish these goals, you establish a cybernetic mindset for both the "I" and the "me."

It is this cybernetic mindset that establishes what behaviors are acceptable and desirable.

This mindset serves as a corrective to maintain your focus: What is my outcome goal and what behaviors do I need to perform in order to accomplish my goal? When you are tempted to stray, the cybernetic visualization works in conjunction with the written goals and provides reinforcement for the behaviors ("I" actions) and ongoing internal evaluations ("me" reports) that help you achieve the greatest level of listening effectiveness.

This is the process of synergy. When you not only behave in a fashion that enables you to listen effectively, but are internally able to evaluate and maintain this behavior consciously then your are being effective. You are in charge of your behavior—a strong internal locus of control. (See Chapter 4 for more on internal locus of control.) This means that you will be more effective when the two parts (the "I" and the "me") work together rather than operating separately or with no direction.

Getting the "I" and the "me" working together has further personal benefits as well. When they work together, it enables you to be productive for greater periods of time. The "me" catches the "I" when your behavior begins to deviate. It allows you to retain greater focus under pressure since you reinforce your goals through visualizing what needs to occur. You also will develop instructions for both parts of your internal nature—the "I" and the "me."

Finally getting the "I" and the "me" working together enables you to better assess your success and your accomplishments because you now have a set of criteria (outcome goals and behaviors by which to meet them) that can be used to measure your achievements, skills, and proficiency. This is another way for you to change behaviors because when you know that you are going to assess results, you will be more careful in the methods used to achieve these results. This is a different way to look at synergism but also a way to help you listen more effectively in meetings!

CHAPTER 33

How Can You Use External Synergy To Stimulate New Ideas?

To list all the dynamic duos who discovered throughout history that two heads are not only better than one, but that two heads hear and do things differently than one would take more space than this entire book. In comedy, Bob Hope always works with a head writer as well as a staff of writers, just as Jay Leno does. In history, Dr. Charles A. and Mrs. Mary Ritter Beard produced at least a dozen histories bearing his name. In scientific research, there is Madame Curie and her husband, and it was Dr. Howard Flory and his wife, also a doctor, who started the flow of penicillin that became a wartime miracle many years ago. Actually a list of names in not that important; it is the principle.

If a list of dynamic duos does not suffice, a list of successful marriages might! If nothing else, the theory that two heads are better than one supports the real benefits of effective marriages. There is no doubt about the benefits of two people working together.

As mentioned in Chapter 7 (*What happens when information is sent through filters?*), we all have filters that screen and modify the information we receive. When we have two heads working on a common project, this becomes very clear—and it doesn't take long! What becomes evident is that what you heard and what the person with you heard, while having some similarities, may be quite different! Sometimes it is radically different! In fact, what you both thought you heard is different. There is no doubt about this fact.

Now, does it mean that one of you heard wrong when you both heard the same thing, but what you report on is quite different? Or was one of you listening more carefully than the other? Perhaps, but

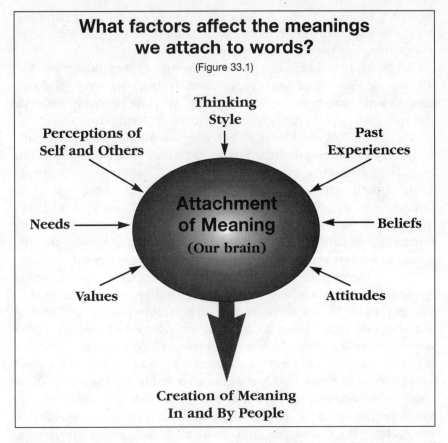

What factors affect the meanings we attach to words?

(Figure 33.1)

Thinking Style

Perceptions of Self and Others

Past Experiences

Attachment of Meaning
(Our brain)

Needs

Beliefs

Values

Attitudes

Creation of Meaning In and By People

more than likely, each of you was filtering different information and listening for different ideas. Our filters affect what we actually think we hear, even though the sounds heard may be identical to the sounds heard by someone else.

In the 1920s, a man by the name of I.A. Richards came up with the idea that meaning is found not within an object but within a person. The words you hear may stimulate different thoughts and different understandings because of your past experiences with those ideas and objects. Because of other's past experiences, these same words may stimulate entirely different thoughts and understandings.

Meaning does not lie in the words themselves. Meaning only lies in the heads of those who hear the words. *(See Figure 33.1.)* It is people who attribute meaning to words, and that is where meaning comes from. This is an extremely important concept in communication because when there is a "communication" breakdown, more often than not it can be traced back to differences in meanings. This becomes a people problem that can be solved simply by making better, more exact, or different language choices to explain ideas, concepts, things or people—whatever.

An example will help clarify the "meaning" explanation. If you had a warm, loving father who appreciated your ideas, work, and successes, when you hear the word "father," you will probably associate meanings such as "compassionate," "affirming," and "supportive."

But if you had an abusive father who was demanding and hostile towards you, when you hear the word "father," you would probably associate meanings such as "animalistic," "angry," or "hurtful." Consequently when the boss uses an analogy about the "company fathers," you may either associate "benevolence" or "fear" with her analogy. Did you hear her incorrectly when she referred to "company fathers?" No, you heard her correctly. You were listening. But the meaning for you was not the same as the one she intended.

This is the point where two heads are better than one. There are numerous situations where you must perform up to your potential so you can reach the best solution, get the most information, or come up with the best ideas. Listening in situations where you are under pressure or stress, for example, may affect your effectiveness. When meeting new clients, you want to make certain you clearly understand what they desire from your company. Listening in situations where there is conflict may affect your effectiveness. When meeting with an employee about to be fired because of incompetence or inability to get along with colleagues, you want to make certain you clearly understand his or her position and his or her feelings. Listening in situations where new ideas are needed may affect your effectiveness. When the company is expanding, or is looking for your expertise and direction, you need to make certain you clearly understand how your assistance can be helpful. What specific input can you provide?

In all these situations, your filters and past associations may prevent you from performing up to your potential. They may prevent you from reaching the best solution or having the best idea. Why? Because even if you are a good listener, you hear and attribute meaning based only upon your own past experience. The aphorism that "you hear what you want to hear" is based on fact. When you introduce a second person, particularly someone you are able to easily relate to, you increase the potential for better understanding of what is being said. Working together, you will be able to come up with different ideas, reach a better solution, or develop a stronger decision. Since the other person will have a different background with different experiences, he or she will attribute meaning differently and consequently will connect different ideas based upon the same information.

This is external synergy in listening. Someone else is listening with you. Someone else is helping you understand things that you might otherwise have missed.

Someone else is introducing ideas to you that you may not have connected. These are cases when you can accomplish more listening with, and through, a second person.

Sometimes we rely too much on just ourselves. We are strong; we are sufficient; we are capable; we can do it ourselves! Self-reliance is the key! But, two heads really can be better than one. Sometimes it takes an experience (like marriage!) to prove it.

Before you try using external synergy, you need to remember one thing: when you choose the other person, make certain he or she is someone who can be honest with you. The second person may be your administrative assistant, your business partner, your spouse, but whomever it is, they must agree to be honest with you. If they are conditioned because of position or prior experience, to tell you what you want to hear, than you have defeated the concept of external synergy before it starts.

The other person must be willing to take a risk and say, "That's not how I heard it at all. What I heard the person saying is..." Realize, of course, that both of you may be right. There actually may be two different versions of reality in this situation. Acknowledge that. Use it to your advantage! Here are four basic ideas for the effective flow of ideas we'd like to leave you with once the two of you get together to combine your thoughts and ideas about what you have heard:

1. Rule out criticism. It only creates arguments.
2. Be as free-wheeling as possible. You are trying to recreate exactly what was said, and often some ideas stimulate other ideas.
3. Strive for quality as well as quantity. In some cases, quality is easy to attain. In others, quality comes from quantity. Use both.
4. Combine and improve on what the other says. It is the ability to hitchhike on other's ideas that gets results. Use the other person as a stimulus, a sounding board, an idea generator, or whatever. Function as if two heads are better than one and you will find that two heads become better than one!

PART NINE

HOW CAN MANAGERS LISTEN FOR PERSONAL GROWTH?

CHAPTER 34

What Does It Mean To "Listen to Yourself"?

After too many days of "learning" I stopped long enough to simply LISTEN. It was then I found that LEARNING is that soft quiet thump beneath the fall of a leaf.
—*Source Unknown*

The question that remains after reading the quotation above is, "What is it that prevents us from hearing the quiet thump beneath the fall of a leaf?" Effective listening is our key to getting at the essential information from which we make decisions and frame ideas for our lives.

The answer to the question is fairly obvious. We are the major factor. We are the ones who prevent ourselves from hearing "the quiet thump beneath the fall of a leaf." This is precisely why effective listening is so difficult. It is habitual behavior and, as pointed out in Chapter 3, habits are deeply rooted within us. Changing attitudes, prejudices, beliefs, values, and behaviors (like listening), even when we realize that it is to our advantage to do so, is difficult. But it is not impossible. If it were, there would be no point in this book!

First, effective listening is vital in all areas of our lives. Business partners split up, employees get fired, husbands and wives divorce, children run away from home, doctors get sued for malpractice, and waitresses bring the wrong order when effective listening doesn't take place. Becoming a more effective listener can increase our levels of self-confidence and personal power. It can accelerate our personal development, increase our intelligence, and improve our personal and professional relationships. By being more sensitive to, more sensible about, and more responsible for the ways we listen, requires that we first understand the value of the process. It can and will make an important difference in our lives. That's the beginning—awareness of the values that effective listening can bring to us.

Second, we must realize that we can do something about poor listening habits. There is no need to withdraw into discouragement or righteousness: "My listening habits have gotten me where I am today. Why should I change them?" Or blaming others: "It's not my fault. If people would only be clear, I would be a better listener!"

Effective listening skills bring out the best in other people. The change is subtle, but it occurs. Changing habits requires effort and constant concentration. It isn't easy, but it can be done. So the second step is recognizing that we can change. We are not doomed to constant failure and inefficiency.

Third, we need to begin paying attention to what is happening within ourselves. What kinds of filters are operating? What barriers do we notice existing within ourselves? Are we being close-minded? It is easy to be open-minded when we agree with the issues. Is our goal to win, or are we seeking information? Are we listening nondefensively? Do we want to control, dominate, and manipulate? We need to pay special attention to our feelings. Are our feelings getting in our way? Are our attitudes, opinions, and beliefs turning others off? Do others think we are able to see both sides of issues?

Fourth, start to develop the characteristics of an effective listener. There is no need to begin all at once. But if we know what the qualities are, slowly and deliberately we can try to incorporate them.

In one of the earliest works on listening, Ralph Nichols, the father of listening, in his dissertation (1948) listed thirteen characteristics of listening:

- alert
- nondistracted
- attending
- nonemotional
- caring
- noninterrupting
- effective evaluator
- understanding
- interested
- responsive
- empathic
- other-centered
- curious
- patient

This task of trying to take on these characteristics may be easier if Dr. Nichols' characteristics of poor listeners are known:

- apathetic
- inattentive
- defensive
- insensitive
- disinterested
- interrupting
- distracted
- quick to judge
- emotional
- self-centered
- impatient
- uncaring

Basically the task of changing poor listening habits comes down to us—how much can we change? It is difficult to focus on what others are saying when we have personal or professional problems. Inner conflicts make effective listening difficult or impossible. Imagine how difficult it is to listen when we have had an argument with a spouse, neighbor, or boss. Anxiety does the same thing. Imagine how difficult it is to listen when we are worried about a forthcoming speech, an IRS audit, or an impending layoff or demotion. In all cases, we cannot concentrate because of lack of energy and inattention.

SUMMARY

What does it mean to "listen to yourself?" Answer the following questions honestly:

1. Do you understand how effective listening can help you?
2. Do you know that you can change poor or ineffective listening habits?
3. Are you willing to monitor your opinions, attitudes, and beliefs to discover the barriers and blocks that are occurring?
4. Are you willing to try to develop the qualities of an effective listener?

This is where change must begin. Our listening habits are learned over a long period of time. To change them is not likely to occur instantly or overnight. We must be patient. But we must also work hard and concentrate on the change that is needed. Only in this way are we likely to hear that soft quiet thump beneath the fall of a leaf.

CHAPTER 35

What Strategies Can You Use For Personal Change?

There are advantages and disadvantages to having listening be a personal process. The advantage is that you have total control over the process. The disadvantage is that if anything is to be done about it, it is *all* up to you and no one else. Remember, it is difficult to change habits—which means it is also easier to forget about trying to change.

We talked about how to change habits in Chapter 3. In talking with a psychiatrist who is engaged in changing habits on a daily basis, we heard him say that behavior change does not occur overnight. What really needs to be done is not to make little changes; what needs to be done is to take off a person's head and put on a new one. His point was simply to reveal how difficult it is to effect change on a permanent basis. Habits are deeply embedded and there are no quick fixes.

In weight gain and weight loss, people experience the same problems as they do when they try to change habits. Why is it, for example, that after losing a substantial amount of weight, it is difficult to keep it off? The body, it seems, has a comfortable weight or form which seems appropriate and proper. After any weight-reduction program, we seem to gain back what was lost. The same is true of habits. We can make changes, but the body wants to return to where it was before the changes in the habits took place. The point is that any change requires constant vigilance to keep that change in place.

What we want to do here is simply establish some of the strategies that form the basis of change in weak or poor listening habits. There are five strategies involved in any process such as this:

Strategy 1

We need to deepen our insight into the causes of our problem. Through the examples in this book, we hope that some of this insight has occurred, but since listening is such a personal process, insight is likely to occur through self-monitoring, self-awareness, and self-actualization. Basically, it is up to us!

Strategy 2

We need to recognize the secret payoffs that may keep us listening ineffectively. Why can't we change? Are we lazy? Is change going to require too much effort and time? Is effective listening going to add to our responsibilities or the demands made upon us? Is there something more beneath the symptoms of ineffective listening? Pain? Anxiety? Depression? Jealousy? Envy? A weak self-concept? Will we feel freer and more independent by not listening well? Often, long-term change and growth means recognizing the cause of the symptoms, letting go of the secret payoffs, and working through the deeper problems we have been avoiding.

Strategy 3

We need to activate our willingness to take responsibility for changing. Once we gain insight into the causes of the problem, once we admit the secret payoffs that have helped us sustain the problem, then we are ready to take charge of overcoming the problem. Poor listening is a problem! And it isn't simply old-fashioned willpower that will help us overcome it. Willpower, by itself, may be too forceful. The problem requires understanding—a true desire to change. This is expressed as a natural, integrated willingness and determination to become the guiding force for change in our own lives. Change begins from within.

Strategy 4

We need to open up our awareness to new ways of thinking, feeling, and acting. Changing a habit as essential as listening, is changing a habit that is closely integrated with our other senses. When we make substantive changes in our listening habits, other changes will occur. As we take the time that effective listening requires, we will notice that we will smell more, see more, feel more, touch more, as well as hear more. All our senses will be activated on a larger scale. We will be affected by a larger number of stimuli. We will actually have a larger amount of information through which we will need to sift to discover the essentials—the messages we need. We need to open up our awareness to the changes that will occur.

Strategy 5

We need to raise our sights to aim at growth and self-actualization. There is a challenge in ineffective listening. It is a challenge that contains the potential for deepening and expansion of our core self. The creative, venturesome risking that changing listening habits requires can only be done from a secure base. That is, you can only endure the kinds of changes we have suggested if you know that you have a core within you that will remain whole and undamaged throughout the process of change. To know and value who you are underneath the problems, joys, ambitions, successes, and worries that form the outer layers of our personality forms the essential foundation from which change occurs. When we have a solid place to stand, we can move adventurously into growth and change.

What is necessary is that we become our own teacher. If we have a problem, it makes sense to depend on the one person who knows the problem, who cares about it, who sees the value of change, who is intimately involved in the process of change, and who is most likely to benefit from what changes take place—ourselves. We care more about our problems and their solutions than anyone else in the world.

SUMMARY

What we need is a system to remind us of the strategies that form the basis of change. If we put these into the form of an intervention strategy it would look like this:

Proper Framework for Change to Occur

4 Be aware of thinking, feeling, and acting.

3 Take responsibility for changing.

2 Recognize secret payoffs that keep us ineffective.

1 Deepen insight into causes of problem.

A Desire to Change Listening Habits

We are not suggesting that this will work for everyone, but we need a starting point. We need to get into the proper mode for change to occur. Changing listening habits is a self-help process. And we need to make full and free use of our own human potential to put effective listening into practice. Only in this way will be able to develop and exercise our full measure of competence—and find pleasure in doing so. Only in this way will we begin to exercise greater self-control and self-direction—and enrich our lives in doing so. Only in this way will we be able to take on additional responsibility and make further commitments—and reap the rewards. These strategies affirm the humanistic vision of the capacity for self-directed growth inherent in all people.

CHAPTER 36

How Does Listening To Yourself Relate To Effectively Listening To Others?

Have you ever sat listening to a speaker and thought to yourself, you could do it better? Have you ever sat in a meeting listening to the group leader and thought to yourself, "I sure hope he lets us out on time?" Have you ever planned for an interview, a sales presentation, or a conflict situation before it actually occurred? In all these situations, you are engaged in a process known as *intrapersonal communication*—the communication you have with yourself. The point here is that this is a process you engage in all the time. It is a comfortable, easy, and ongoing process. Doing it more effectively will improve your effectiveness in listening to others.

Listening to yourself relates to effectively listening to others because by listening to yourself you remove some of the barriers that impede and restrict your ability to listen to others. That is, by listening to yourself you become aware of what you are doing and aware, too, of what you can do better. You can check to see how successful you are when listening to others; that is, you can monitor how sensitive you are and how sensitively you respond. What we are suggesting is that this new sensitivity should be clear and obvious—especially in contrast to the way you listened before.

There are numerous ways in which this sensitivity is revealed. Many of the following ideas are obvious, but they need to be mentioned since each can become a goal as well as a characteristic of our listening behavior. The problem with listening is that it is a commonplace problem, and the solutions are commonplace as well. But why don't we listen well? It is because we take the process for granted. As commonplace as the following ideas are, we need constant reminders about their importance and relevance.

How do we listen sensibly and sensitively? In their book *Effective Listening: Key to Your Success*, Steil, Barker, and Watson (1983) note ten guidelines for effective listening. They, like many of the other authors noted in our bibliography, have found these elements to be critical if we are to listen effectively. We have expanded on these core ideas to offer the following suggestions:

1. We must maintain mental energy. Effective listening takes energy and work. Many people have short attention spans. They are willing to listen, but they listen only for a short time. Others, just because of poor training, a relaxed comfortable disposition, the unwillingness to be taxed or challenged, or tiredness, either never engage others through listening or simply tune out when the need to listen occurs. Effective listeners are able to tap their internal resources. Can we draw together the mental and physical strength necessary to listen to others?

2. We must view topics as interesting. As soon as a topic is considered uninteresting, we tend to turn off our attention and our willingness to listen. There is a tendency to prejudge subjects as uninteresting, dull, dry, or boring (i.e., the meeting where attendance is mandatory, a training seminar, the employer's state of the business report, etc.) Who cares? In every situation there is something we may be able to make use of in the future. We need to listen selfishly by asking, "What's in this for me?" Effective listeners train themselves to find areas of interest and concern. Ask yourself, "How can I make the best of it and get the most from any situation?"

3. Do not be distracted by delivery. It is too easy to let a person's monotone, lack of movement, distracting appearance, or repetitive gestures divert us from the content. Effective listeners overlook or repress negative aspects of people's delivery or appearance to concentrate on the message. There is a tendency to

remember the delivery rather than the message. Effective listeners focus on the content. How can we best concentrate and eliminate distractions?

4. We must control our emotional reactions. When we dislike other people, when we disagree with their viewpoint, or when we object to their content, we let our emotions take control. What happens is that we allow our internal reactions to control our responses. We may make internal refutations; we may prepare our own responses; or we may turn others off entirely. Effective listeners withhold judgment. How can we fully receive and understand first so that our judgment is likely to be appropriate later?

5. We must meet the challenge of difficult information. Many people do not have much practice listening to difficult material. When they anticipate difficulty, they turn off and tune out others. Difficult information places a heavy demand on people's mental energy. Managers may want to wait for a follow-up explanation, for the full written report, or for a condensed version. Effective listeners listen even when not motivated to do so. Are we willing to seek out difficult and complex listening situations?

6. We must try not to organize everything. In some cases, organizing prevents us from listening simply because others have not organized their information. Sometimes it hinders listening because we impose our own organizational scheme on information that is organized differently. Sometimes, too, it causes us to look for too many details—trying to flesh out the outline. Listen for a short time, and record key ideas and concepts. Effective listeners take notes. How can we best adapt to the organizational schemes of others?

7. We must maintain attention. Most people have become quite skilled in faking attention. They can pretend to listen. These people fake eye contact, head nods, facial expressions, and other signals like shifting their weight, or maintaining an erect posture to signal that they are listening. Faking can become a habit. Some are so good at this that they take short mental journeys without realizing they are no longer paying attention.

They are easily carried away by a thought, word, or phrase. Effective listeners are attentive. Can you remember what others have said?

8. We must control, adjust to, or compensate for distractions. There are few listening situations in which distractions are not present. For example, there is likely to be music, movement, other people, and outside noise in almost all listening situations. In a business environment, we are likely to find the sounds of telephones, computer printers, conversations, and normal traffic around the office. In many cases, we cannot modify these environmental conditions. Of course, when we can, we should. But when we cannot, we must modify internal conditions—what happens within ourselves. Effective listeners are aware of distractions. Can you compensate for distractions by evaluating, anticipating, reviewing, or summarizing others' information?

9. We must listen holistically. Often, we tend to listen just for the facts. Managers who listen just for the facts try to get to the bottom line: *when* are the papers to be submitted; *how many* copies need to be completed; at *what* time are they needed; and *where* is the material to be delivered? These facts can be written down and reviewed later. Often, that is precisely why we are driven by the need for facts. But listening just for facts may prevent analysis and evaluation. The essence of the message may be in its purpose, the setting, its structure, or the nature of the message. These are items needed for proper interpretation. Effective listeners listen for the whole message. How can you gain a better understanding of all the parts and how they fit into the complete message?

10. Capitalize on *thought speed.* People think at a rate in excess of 600 words per minute. Most people talk at a rate of 150 to 200 words per minute. When others talk, our thoughts will run well beyond their words. This is why it is easy to take short mental journeys; we have time to think. Effective listeners use their thought speed constructively. To what extent do you anticipate, review, summarize, and evaluate what has been said to keep your mind focused on the message?

These ten items from Steil, Barker and Watson (1983) do not guarantee effectiveness. There are no guarantees. But they can serve as both characteristics of effective listeners as well as goals for which you can strive.

SUMMARY

We are not saying that these are the only suggestions for effective listening that will aid personal growth. We also are not suggesting they are mutually exclusive. They are likely to overlap. These suggestions will provide specific ideas about what you can do to improve your listening skills. They also will give you specific areas to monitor as you seek greater effectiveness. The ultimate success in effective listening is gaining more information. Through attaining more information, personal improvement results.

Here we will simply review the specific questions that will allow you to analyze your effectiveness. Prior to practicing these skills, it might be helpful for you to prepare and commit yourself to *active listening*. If possible, think about the topic and situation in advance. Try to match your listening goals with those brought by the speaker to the situation. Use these questions as a guide to winning at listening:

1. Can you draw together the mental and physical strength necessary to listen to others?
2. How can you make the best of, and get the most from, any situation?
3. How can you best concentrate and eliminate distractions?
4. How can you fully receive and understand information first so that your judgment is likely to be appropriate later?
5. Are you willing to seek out difficult and complex listening situations?
6. How can you best adapt to the organizational scheme of others? Can you remember what others have said?
8. Can you compensate for distractions by evaluating, anticipating, reviewing, or summarizing others' information?

9. How can you gain a better understanding of all the parts of another's message and how they fit into the complete message?
10. To what extent do you anticipate, review, summarize, and evaluate what has been said to keep your mind focused on the message?

To put these ideas into action, we need to constantly remind ourselves that effective listening is vital to effective communication. Effective communication is vital to personal success. And personal success will result in happiness both at home and in the workplace.

Listen to win.

References

Barker, L. (1971). *Listening Behavior*. Englewood Cliffs, NJ: Prentice-Hall.

Bennett, J. C., & Olney, R. J. (1986). Executive priorities for effective communication in an information society. *The Journal of Business Communication, 23*(2), 13-22.

Binder, E. F., & McGone, E. L. (1971). Experimental evaluation of the Xerox effective listening course. *Western Speech, 35,* 264-270.

Booth-Butterfield, M. (1984). She hears...he hears: What they hear and why. *Personnel Journal, 63*(5), 36-42.

Bostrom, Robert N. (1990). *Listening Behavior: Measurement and Application*. New York: The Guilford Press.

Brownell, J. (1984). Listening: A powerful management tool. *Supervisory Management, 29*(10), 35-39.

Cahn, D. (1974). Perceived understanding, supervisor-subordinate communication, and organizational effectiveness. *Central States Speech Journal, 25,* 19-26.

Curtis, D. B., Winsor, J. L., & Stephens, R. D. (1989). National preferences in business and communication education. *Communication Education, 38,* 6-14.

DiSalvo, V. S. (1980). A summary of current research identifying communication skills in various organizational contexts. *Communication Education, 29,* 283-290.

Eisenhart, T. (1989, January). You're talking—but are they listening? *Business Marketing,* 30-37.

Floyd, J. J., & Reese, R. G. (1987). Listening theory in modern rhetorical thought. *Journal of the International Listening Association, 1,* 87-102.

Hunt, G., & Cusella, L. P. (1983). A field study of listening needs in organizations. *Communication Education, 32,* 393 -401.

Jablin, F. M., Putnam, L. L., Roberts, K. H., & Porter, L. W. (1989). *Handbook of Organizational Communication*. Newbury Park, CA: SAGE.

Kelly, C. (1967). Listening: A complex of activities or a unitary skill? *Speech Monographs, 34,* 455-466.

Labich, K. (1988, October). The seven keys to business leadership. *Fortune,* pp. 58-66.

Lewis, M. H., & Reinsch, N. L. (1988). Listening in organizational environments. *The Journal of Business Communication, 25*(3), 49-67.

Litterst, J. K., & Eyo, B. (1982). Gauging the effectiveness of formal communication programs: A search for the communication-productivity link. *The Journal of Business Communication, 19*(2), 15-25.

McClelland, V. A. (1988). Standard communication: Is anyone listening? *Personnel Journal, 67*(6), 124–129.

Meister, J. E., & Reinsch, N. L. (1978). Communication training in manufacturing firms. *Communication Education, 27,* 235-244.

Morgan, P., & Baker, K. H. (1985). Building a professional image: Improving listening behavior. *Supervisory Management, 30,* 34-38.

Nichols, R. (1957). Are you listening? New York: McGraw-Hill.

Peters, T., & Austin, N. (1985). MBWA (management by walking around). *California Management Review, 28*(1), 9-34 .

Rhodes, S. (1985, July). *Listening perceived to be important for effective organizational communication: A preliminary study.* Paper presented at the Second Annual International Listening Association Summer Conference, Minneapolis, MN.

Richmond, V. P., McCroskey, J. C., & Davis, L. M. (1986). The relationship of supervisor use of power and affinity-seeking strategies with subordinate satisfaction. *Communication Quarterly, 32*(2), 178-193.

Smeltzer, L. R., & Watson, K. (1988). A test of instructional strategies for listening improvement in a simulated business setting. *The Journal of Business Communication, 22*(4), 33-42.

Steil, L. K., Barker, L. L., & Watson, K. W. (1983). *Effective listening : Key to your success.* Reading: Addison-Wesley.

Sypher, B. D., Bostrum, R. N., & Seibert, J. H. (1989). Listening, communication abilities, and success at work. *The Journal of Business Communication, 26*(4), 293-303.

Weaver, R. L. II (1993). *Understanding Interpersonal Communication,* 6th ed. New York: HarperCollins.

Weinrauch, D. J., & Swanda, J. R. (1976). Examining the significance of listening: An exploratory study of contemporary management. *The Journal of Business Communication, 13*(1), 25-32.

About the Authors

Curt Bechler is a professor at Denison University. Besides his work on the subject of listening, Bechler specializes in organizational communication, with a research emphasis on team and crisis communication. His consulting group, Bechler Communication International, works with both nonprofit and profit groups on issues related to communication effectiveness.

Before becoming a professor at Denison University, he spent ten years working as an administrator at a camp and conference center in southern Michigan.

Bechler and his wife, Shari, are avid backpackers and beachcombers who make their home in Newark, Ohio.

Richard L. Weaver II is a professor in the Department of Interpersonal Communication at Bowling Green State University. His books include the best-selling *Understanding Interpersonal Communication* and *Communicating Effectively* (with Saundra Hybels), as well as *Understanding Business Communication* and *Research in Speech Communication.* He is a long-time contributor to the professional journals in his field, and he has received a number of outstanding teaching awards, including Bowling Green's Faculty Excellence Award.

Weaver received his undergraduate and master's degrees from the University of Michigan and his doctorate degree from Indiana University. He has taught at the University of Massachusetts, the University of Hawaii, five different universities in Australia, and for twenty years at Bowling Green. He is a frequent speaker at universities, conferences, and professional organizations. Ten of his speeches have been published in *Vital Speeches of the Day.*

Weaver has four grown children and resides in Perrysburg, Ohio, with his wife, Andrea.

Copies of *Listen To Win* may be ordered by sending a check for $18.95 to MasterMedia Limited, 17 East 89th Street, New York, NY 10128. Or call (800) 334-8232 or fax (212) 546-7638. Please include $2 for postage and handling of the first copy, $1 for each additional copy.

MasterMedia's authors are available for speeches and seminars. Please contact Tony Colao, speaker's bureau director, at (800) 453-2887 or fax (908) 359-1647.

Other MasterMedia Books

AGING PARENTS AND YOU: A Complete Handbook to Help You Help Your Elders Maintain a Healthy, Productive, Independent Life, by Eugenia Anderson-Ellis, is a complete guide to providing care to aging relatives. It features practical advice and resources for adults helping their elders lead productive lives. Revised and updated. ($9.95 paper)

BALANCING ACTS! Juggling Love, Work, Family, and Recreation, by Susan Stautberg and Marcia L. Worthing, provides strategies to achieve a balanced life by reordering priorities and setting realistic goals. ($12.95 paper)

BEATING THE AGE GAME, Redefining Retirement, by Jack and Phoebe Ballard, debunks the myth that retirement means sitting out the rest of the game. The years between 55 and 80 can be your best, say the authors, who provide ample examples of people successfully using retirement to reinvent their lives. ($12.95 paper)

BEYOND SUCCESS: How Volunteer Service Can Help You Begin Making a Life Instead of Just a Living, by John J. Raynolds III and Eleanor Raynolds, C.B.E., is a unique how-to book targeted at business and professional people considering volunteer work, senior citizens who wish to fill leisure time meaningfully, and students trying out career options. ($9.95 paper, $19.95 cloth)

THE BIG APPLE BUSINESS AND PLEASURE GUIDE: 501 Ways To Work Smarter, Play Harder, and Live Better in New York City, by Muriel Siebert and Susan Kleinman, offers visitors and New Yorkers alike advice on how to do business in the city as well as how to enjoy its attractions. ($9.95 paper)

BREATHING SPACE: Living and Working at a Comfortable Pace in a Sped-up Society, by Jeff Davidson, helps readers to handle information and activity overload, in order to gain greater control over their lives. ($10.95 paper)

CITIES OF OPPORTUNITY: Finding the Best Way to Work, Live, and Prosper in the 1990s and Beyond, by Dr. John Tepper Martin, explores the job and living options for the next decade and into the next century. This consumer guide and handbook, written by one of the world's experts on cities, selects and features forty-six American cities and metropolitan areas. ($13.95 paper, $24.95 cloth)

THE CONFIDENCE FACTOR: How Self-Esteem Can Change Your Life, by Dr. Judith Briles, is based on a nationwide survey of six thousand men and women. Briles explores why women so often feel a lack of self-confidence and have a poor opinion of themselves. She offers step-by-step advice on becoming the person you want to be. ($12.95 paper, $18.95 cloth)

DARE TO CONFRONT! How To Intervene When Someone You Care About Has a Drug or Alcohol Problem, by Bob Wright and Deborah George Wright, shows the reader how to use the step-by-step methods of professional interventionists to motivate drug-dependent people to accept help they need. ($17.95 cloth)

THE DOLLARS AND SENSE OF DIVORCE: The Financial Guide for Women, by Dr. Judith Briles, is the first book to combine the legal hurdles by planning finances before, during, and after divorce. ($10.95 paper)

THE ENVIRONMENTAL GARDENER: The Solution to Pollution for Lawns and Gardens, by Laurence Sombke, focuses on what each of us can do to protect our endangered plant life. A practical source book and shopping guide. ($8.95 paper)

FINANCIAL SAVVY FOR WOMEN: A Money Book for Women of All Ages, by Dr. Judith Briles, divides a woman's monetary life span into six phases, discusses specific issues to be addressed at each stage, and demonstrates how to create a sound money plan. ($15.00 paper)

FLIGHT PLAN FOR LIVING: The Art of Self-Encouragement, by Patrick O'Dooley, is a life guide organized like a pilot's checklist, to ensure you'll be flying "clear on top" throughout your life. ($17.95 cloth)

GLORIOUS ROOTS: Recipes for Healthy, Tasty Vegetables, by Laurence Sombke, celebrates the taste, texture, and versatility of root vegetables. Contains recipes for appetizers, soups, stews, and baked, broiled, and stir-fried dishes—even desserts. ($12.95 paper)

HOT HEALTH-CARE CAREERS, by Margaret T. McNally, R.N., and Phyllis Schneider, provides readers everything they need to know about training for and getting jobs in a rewarding field where professionals are always in demand. ($10.95 paper)

HOW TO GET WHAT YOU WANT FROM ALMOST ANYBODY, by T. Scott Gross, shows how to get great service, negotiate better prices, and always get what you pay for. ($9.95 paper)

KIDS WHO MAKE A DIFFERENCE, by Joyce M. Roché and Marie Rodriguez, is an inspiring document of how today's toughest challenges are being met by teenagers and kids, whose courage and creativity enables them to find practical solutions! ($8.95 paper, with photos)

THE LIVING HEART BRAND NAME SHOPPER'S GUIDE, by Michael E. DeBakey, M.D., Antonio M. Gotto, Jr., M.D., Lynne W. Scott, M.A., R.D./L.D., and John P. Foreyt, Ph.D., lists brand name products low in fat, saturated fatty acids, and cholesterol. Revised edition. ($14.95 paper)

THE LIVING HEART GUIDE TO EATING OUT, by Michael E. DeBakey, Antonio M. Gotto, Jr., and Lynne W. Scott, is an essential handbook for people who want to maintain a health-conscious diet when dining in all types of restaurants. ($9.95 paper)

THE LOYALTY FACTOR: Building Trust in Today's Workplace, by Carol Kinsey Goman, Ph.D., offers techniques for restoring commitment and loyalty in the workplace. ($9.95 paper)

MAKING YOUR DREAMS COME TRUE: A Plan For Easily Discovering and Achieving the Life You Want, by Marcia Wieder, introduces an easy, unique, and practical technique for defining, pursuing, and realizing your career and life interests. Filled with stories of real people and helpful exercises, plus a personal workbook. ($9.95 paper)

MANAGING IT ALL: Time-Saving Ideas for Career, Family, Relationships, and Self, by Beverly Benz Treuille and Susan Schiffer Stautberg, is written for women juggling careers and families. With interviews of more than two hundred career women (ranging from a TV anchorwoman to an investment banker), this book contains many humorous anecdotes on saving time and improving the quality of life. ($9.95 paper)

MANAGING YOUR PSORIASIS, by Nicholas J. Lowe, M.D., is an innovative manual that couples scientific research and encouraging support, with an emphasis on how patients can take charge of their health. ($10.95 paper, $17.95 cloth)

MANN FOR ALL SEASONS: Wit and Wisdom from The Washington Post's *Judy Mann,* shows the columnist at her best as she writes about women, families, and the impact and politics of the women's revolution. ($9.95 paper, $19.95 cloth)

MIND YOUR OWN BUSINESS: And Keep it in the Family, by Marcy Syms, CEO of Syms Corp, is an effective guide for any organization facing the toughest step in managing a family business—making the transition to the new generation. ($12.95 paper, $18.95 cloth)

OFFICE BIOLOGY: Why Tuesday Is the Most Productive Day and Other Relevant Facts for Survival in the Workplace, by Edith Weiner and Arnold Brown, teaches how in the '90s and beyond we will be expected to work smarter, take better control of our health, adapt to advancing technology, and improve our lives in ways that are not too costly or resource-intensive. ($12.95 paper, $21.95 cloth)

ON TARGET: Enhance Your Life and Advance Your Career, by Jeri Sedlar and Rick Miners, is a neatly woven tapestry of insights on career and life issues gathered from audiences across the country. This feedback has been crystallized into a highly readable guide for exploring who you are and how to go about getting what you want. ($11.95 paper)

OUT THE ORGANIZATION: New Career Opportunities for the 1990s, by Robert and Madeleine Swain, is written for the millions of Americans whose jobs are no longer safe, whose companies are not loyal, and who face futures of uncertainty, provides advice on finding a new job or starting your own business. (Revised $12.95 paper, $17.95 cloth)

THE OUTDOOR WOMAN: A Handbook to Adventure, by Patricia Hubbard and Stan Wass, details the lives of adventurous women and offers their ideas on how you can incorporate exciting outdoor experiences into your life. ($14.95 paper)

PAIN RELIEF: How to Say No to Acute and Chronic Pain, by Dr. Jane Cowles, offers a step-by-step plan for assessing pain and communicating it to your doctor, and explains the importance of having a pain plan before undergoing any medical or surgical treatment; includes "The Pain Patient's Bill of Rights," and a reusable pain assessment chart. ($22.95 paper)

POSITIVELY OUTRAGEOUS SERVICE: New and Easy Ways To Win Customers for Life, by T. Scott Gross, identifies what '90s consumers really want and how business can develop effective marketing strategies to answer those needs. ($14.95 paper)

POSITIVELY OUTRAGEOUS SERVICE AND SHOWMANSHIP, by T. Scott Gross, reveals the secrets of adding personality to any product or service and offers a wealth of nontraditional marketing techniques employed by top showmen, from car dealers to restaurateurs, amusement park operators to evangelists. ($12.95 paper)

THE PREGNANCY AND MOTHERHOOD DIARY: Planning the First Year of Your Second Career, by Susan Schiffer Stautberg, is only undated appointment diary that shows how to manage pregnancy and career. ($12.95 spiral)

REAL BEAUTY…REAL WOMEN: A Handbook for Making the Best of Your Own Good Looks, by Kathleen Walas, International Beauty and Fashion Director of Avon Products, Inc., offers expert advice on beauty and fashion for women of all ages and ethnic backgrounds. ($19.95 paper)

REAL LIFE 101: The Graduate's Guide To Survival, by Susan Kleinman, supplies welcome advice to those facing "real life" for the first time, focusing on work, money, health, and how to deal with freedom and responsibility. Revised. ($9.95 paper)

ROSEY GRIER'S ALL-AMERICAN HEROES: Multicultural Success Stories, by Roosevelt "Rosey" Grier, is a candid collection of profiles of prominent African Americans, Latins, Asians, and Native Americans who revealed how they achieved public acclaim and personal success. ($9.95 paper, with photos)

SELLING YOURSELF: How To Be the Competent, Confident Person You Really Are! by Kathy Thebo and Joyce Newman, is an inspirational primer for anyone seeking to project a positive image. Drawing on experience, their own and others', these entrepreneurs offer simple techniques that can add up to big successes. ($11.95 paper)

SHOCKWAVES: The Global Impact of Sexual Harassment, by Susan L. Webb, examines the problem of sexual harassment today in every kind of workplace around the world. Practical and well-researched, this manual provides the most recent information available, including legal changes in progress. ($11.95 paper, $19.95 cloth)

SIDE-BY-SIDE STRATEGIES: How Two-Career Couples Can Thrive in the '90s, by Jane Hershey Cuozzo and S. Diane Graham, describes how to learn the difference between competing with a spouse and become a supportive power partner. Published in hardcover as Power Partners. ($10.95 paper, $19.95 cloth)

THE SOLUTION TO POLLUTION: 101 Things You Can Do To Clean Up Your Environment, by Laurence Sombke, offers step-by-step techniques on how to conserve more energy, start a recycling center, choose a biodegradable product, and proceed with individual clean-up projects. ($7.95 paper)

THE SOLUTION TO POLLUTION IN THE WORKPLACE, by Laurence Sombke, Terry M. Robertson, and Elliot M. Kaplan, offers everything employees need to know about cleaning up their workplace, including recycling, using energy efficiently, conserving water, and buying nontoxic supplies. ($9.95 paper)

SOMEONE ELSE'S SON, by Alan A. Winter, explores the parent-child bond in a contemporary novel of lost identities, family secrets, and relationships gone awry. Eighteen years after bringing their first son home from the hospital, Trish and Brad Hunter discover they are not his biological parents. ($18.95 cloth)

STEP FORWARD: Sexual Harassment in the Workplace, by Susan L. Webb, presents the facts for dealing with sexual harassment on the job. ($9.95 paper)

THE STEPPARENT CHALLENGE: A Primer For Making It Work, by Stephen J. Williams, Ph.D., offers insight into the many aspects of step relationships—from financial issues to lifestyle changes to differences in race or religion that affect the whole family. ($13.95 paper)

STRAIGHT TALK ON WOMEN'S HEALTH: How to Get the Health Care You Deserve, by Janice Teal, Ph.D., and Phyllis Schneider, is destined to become a health-care "bible." Devoid of confusing medical jargon, it offers a wealth of resources, including contact lists of healthlines and women's medical centers. ($14.95 paper)

TAKING CONTROL OF YOUR LIFE: The Secrets of Successful Enterprising Women, by Gail Blanke and Kathleen Walas, is based on the authors' professional experience with Avon Products' Women of Enterprise Awards, given each year to outstanding female entrepreneurs; offers a plan to help you gain control over your life, plus business tips as well as beauty and lifestyle information. ($17.95 cloth)

TEAMBUILT: Making Teamwork Work, by Mark Sanborn, teaches businesses how to increase productivity, without increasing resources or expenses, by building teamwork among employees. ($12.95 paper, $19.95 cloth)

A TEEN'S GUIDE TO BUSINESS: The Secrets to a Successful Enterprise, by Linda Menzies, Oren S. Jenkins, and Rick R. Fisher, provides solid information about starting your own business or working for one. ($7.95 paper)

TWENTYSOMETHING: Managing & Motivating Today's New Work Force, by Lawrence J. Bradford, Ph.D., and Claire Raines, M.A., examines the work orientation of the younger generation and offers managers practical advice for understanding and supervising their young employees. ($12.95 paper, $22.95 cloth)

WHAT KIDS LIKE TO DO, by Edward Stautberg, Gail Wubbenhorst, Atiya Easterling, and Phyllis Schneider, is a handy guide for parents, grandparents, and baby sitters. Written by kids for kids, this is an easy-to-read, generously illustrated primer for teaching families how to make every day more fun. ($7.95 paper)